Conversations with Dad

A life well lived

SUZIE MORWOOD

A DIVISION OF HAY HOUSE

Copyright © 2022 Suzie Morwood.

All rights reserved. No part of this book may be used or reproduced by any means, graphic, electronic, or mechanical, including photocopying, recording, taping or by any information storage retrieval system without the written permission of the author except in the case of brief quotations embodied in critical articles and reviews.

Balboa Press books may be ordered through booksellers or by contacting:

Balboa Press
A Division of Hay House
1663 Liberty Drive
Bloomington, IN 47403
www.balboapress.com
844-682-1282

Because of the dynamic nature of the Internet, any web addresses or links contained in this book may have changed since publication and may no longer be valid. The views expressed in this work are solely those of the author and do not necessarily reflect the views of the publisher, and the publisher hereby disclaims any responsibility for them.

The author of this book does not dispense medical advice or prescribe the use of any technique as a form of treatment for physical, emotional, or medical problems without the advice of a physician, either directly or indirectly. The intent of the author is only to offer information of a general nature to help you in your quest for emotional and spiritual well-being. In the event you use any of the information in this book for yourself, which is your constitutional right, the author and the publisher assume no responsibility for your actions.

Any people depicted in stock imagery provided by Getty Images are models, and such images are being used for illustrative purposes only. Certain stock imagery © Getty Images.

Scripture quotations marked NIV are taken from the Holy Bible, New International Version®. NIV®. Copyright © 1973, 1978, 1984 by International Bible Society. Used by permission of Zondervan. All rights reserved. [Biblica]

Print information available on the last page.

ISBN: 979-8-7652-3530-0 (sc)
ISBN: 979-8-7652-3531-7 (e)

Balboa Press rev. date: 11/30/2022

DEDICATION

I would like to dedicate this book in the memory of my mother Margaret Ida as a tribute to my dad.

CONTENTS

Acknowledgment ix
Foreword xi
About the Author xiii
About the Book xv

Chapter 1   My father's character 1
Chapter 2   Rules he lived by 5
Chapter 3   Life without Mother 13
Chapter 4   His strength and High energy 17
Chapter 5   Remembering Ole Granny. And trips to Boston 21
Chapter 6   Vacations with my family 29
Chapter 7   Road trip across Canada 35
Chapter 8   Pandemic and Isolation 39
Chapter 9   Paris trip with the Kiwanis. 45
Chapter 10   Friends and Humor 51
Chapter 11   College of St, Ann's Digby NS 57
Chapter 12   Always wanted to be a salesman! 63
Chapter 13   Fond Memories of the Past 67
Chapter 14   Always a true supporter of me! 73
Chapter 15   MicMac Street 79
Chapter 16   Courting my mom 85
Chapter 17   Conversations with my dad Last chapter 93

ACKNOWLEDGMENT

One of the truly joyous parts of writing a book is thanking those who have so kindly contributed to the development and finally the completion of this book.

My reason for writing this book in the first place is to leave a small legacy for my children and grandchildren of the man they knew as father, grandfather and great grandfather. These are the memories I have unfolded of my dad. He truly means a lot to me.

Firstly I want to thank my dad for being the star attraction of this book. He played the most important role. There were many evening I would call dad long distance and ask him questions about the family with whom he grew up. He told me many stories and he is still telling me stories, some he repeats because he has a different twist on the original.

Secondly I want to thank my husband Frank for giving me so much encouragement and also helping me to remember some the stories that he was told by my dad.

Thank you Sandy Crawford for also encouraging me to finish this project and also for writing the introduction to the book.

FOREWORD

A Story Teller's Story

Let me introduce you to the author, Suzie Morwood, and briefly therefore, to Pa. She will tell you his story. Over the years, I've had the honour of appreciating both these adventurers extremely well, and I can assure you, the wanderlust genetics were definitely passed down through the generations. Suzie and I knew, when we first met, our paths were meant to cross and we would be Sister Friends forever. I have revelled, belly laughed and joined in many of the shenanigans of this fun loving woman with the heart of a kid. This energetic soul keeps me laughing, with her raucous sense of humour, while I've cheered her on in her ambitions and dreams, as well as sometimes shaking my head in disbelief at her whirlwind of exciting exits and entrances. She has always appealed to the wild in my soul, whether it was boldly standing in the pouring rain, grinning while eating our soggy sandwiches at Kanaka Creek, British Columbia, beside the voyageur canoe, or desperately running down dark, dusty, dangerous, crazy crowded night streets in Delhi, India, following a wild rickshaw carrying her wonderful daughter, Jessica, and grandson, while trying to catch our bus on time. We've definitely had an abundance of tremendous adventures. All of these memories still make my heart smile.

Suzie has always been up to a challenge. 'Adventure' is definitely her middle name, which she lives up to. She and Pa share the belief that "It's not over til it's over", so make every moment count and keep dancing to the music of life with every breath you have. She believes that everyone needs to believe in themselves and has always encouraged me in my endeavours. Whenever I'm looking for a new adventure Suzie's number is at the top of my list.

The author started her life in Halifax, born with wide eyed wonder. Since then she has eagerly travelled coast to coast many times over the years, as well as India and Spain and a number of other places, along with numerous steps and stories along the way. Throughout her life, whenever this spunky woman has travelled, she has been welcomed for her vibrant self, and has made many life long friends along the highway of life. This explorer continued her education later in life, becoming a nurse and working that profession for years. She has achieved an entire array of goals, from getting her doctorate in religious counselling to learning Spanish, as just a few of her accomplishments. It's obvious she is definitely not finished with sampling new experiences and enjoying the smorgasbord of life. And now, here is her second book. She writes in this book of her father's adventures and her experiences with her dad.

The wonderful thing is that her father also took me in as family and has always made me feel welcome as part of the family. I have always called him Pa, with the utmost of respect and affection. Suzie wrote this memoir of her father's experiences and influences, with the goal of having his life shared and live on as a legacy for her amazing daughters and grandchildren, who, along with her devoted husband, she is dedicated to. With Pa's wanderlust, his zest and energetic passion for life, and his robust sense of humour, I admire that he has always been up to a challenge in life, and has always jumped right in to try novel experiences.

Therefore, I know you'll enjoy these warm hearted adventures of Pa's life. So sit back and prepare to be entertained and inspired. The author has a deep love and respect for her father and this is a tribute to him.

By Sandy Crawford

ABOUT THE AUTHOR

Suzie Morwood presents here with a brief window into her world. She has created this memoir as a legacy for her family. She has accomplished a lot in her life from selling sunglasses as a child to becoming a psychiatric nurse and later a doctorate in counselling. This is her second book her first is another memoir called Sunglasses 25 cents. She lives with her husband of many years in eastern Canada.

ABOUT THE BOOK

It is a story of a man who lived his life well and pure of heart. A man who wouldn't hurt anyone then. I guess you can tell already that I love my dad. A wonderfully loving and uniquely special man; this is what my friend Sandy says about him. I tend to agree. The conversations with me and my dad are from his memory in his late 90s. He has a lot of great stories to tell.

My dad - The man who was the authority figure in our home, was brought up in a house with similar beliefs that I had. I never really knew his parents- not sure why. I will never know since all the family is gone except my dad and his two nephews. Dad finds it very difficult to talk about his family. So, the story will be about how he impacted my life and those around him. I am reflecting on him and all he was in my life. It is also important to note that my mother was an essential part of his life, so my mother will be part of the story from time to time. They were married for almost 72 years and went everywhere together and discussed everything. Having said this, it is primarily about my dad.

I can remember my dad being a great and strong man who supported his children- my brother and me with immense love. He was a quiet man with an extensive and imposing voice. When he spoke, it was with authority and power. He was not always around when I was a young child as he was traveling as a salesman.

Yes, my dad was a salesman, so my mother was the disciplinarian in our household. He was around for most of my brother's growing-up years. We moved to Saint John, New Brunswick when my brother was eight years old and I was fifteen. This is a brief look into my dad's life.

CHAPTER 1

My father's character

I have always compared my dad's personality to our heavenly Father, loving and compassionate. Our Heavenly Father is not unkind and cruel but loving and passionate towards all his children. Our Heavenly Father longs to have loving relationships with all his children on earth. It is exactly what my dad longed for all his life. Not that my dad is God, but he indeed does have compassion for all.

My dad was a good provider throughout his life. I had no idea as a child how that all worked. Dad would go away for a week at a time. We got an allowance on the 15th of every month. We would get an allowance, and the family would go grocery shopping on Saturdays. My mom didn‹t do any job after my brother‹s birth. So, my dad was the only provider.

I always longed for my birthday. It is on the 15th of January, which meant I would get a present since that was dad‹s payday. In the Gospel, we are encouraged to call Father God Abba; Abba is an Aramaic word meaning Farther, which conveys a sense of warm intimacy and respect for the father. It is equivalent to saying «Papa». (NIV Nave‹s Topical Bible).

Many of us have been raised to think of our Father as fearsome and punishing without any reason. But to those who follow him and love him, he is our loving Papa- like every wonderful parent should be. I am not lying; my dad was and still is all of the above. I only remember once my dad was provoked by my sibling's misbehavior, and he wanted to correct him, but my mother and grandmother interfered - "don't touch him" still rings in my ears.

So many of my conversations with dad once my mom passed seem to reflect on his relationship with her. We will chat about his childhood and then be redirected by dad, of course. Oh, I miss my mom so much. It has been a great time of contemplation for Dad. He has been totally devoted to his mom and his wife, the same. It has been more challenging to write a story of us without including mom from time to time.

I have so many great memories of my dad and my mom. We, the three us, had a special bond. So often, the two of them always asked about my husband why didn't frank come? Or how is Frank, or Poor Frank, became a family cliche. Primarily my maternal grandmother used to call my husband, Poor Frank.

Dad always had a book in his hand

CHAPTER 2

Rules he lived by

I have found three verses in the bible that relate to parenting, mentioning them below with how I was raised. Not everyone reading this portion of the book will appreciate the comparison, so my apologies.

Fathers, do not provoke your children to anger but bring them up in the discipline and instruction of the Lord Ephesians 6:4

When I first found this verse and pondered how I could apply it to my life with my dad and growing up, I thought I just had to keep from making my children angry. But that's not what the verse means. "Provoke" here is intended as "avoiding unfair and cruel behavior" or "blatant favoritism."

Since I have two children, it makes sense that I should avoid cruel situations or show favoritism to one child over the other. It isn't easy to play favorites, but it was never the intention to do so. I love both of my children the exact amount, but I don't treat them the same. They were two different people with two other dreams, and I needed to discipline them.

According to that standard, each child looks at how they were treated, not at the reason why it was best for them. So, we thought that parents only learn from the example of their upbringing or a book. A few of my friends followed the teaching of Dr. Spock, The Common-Sense Book of Baby and Child Care. But children always want to compare how they are treated differently from their siblings. They only saw what was done for the other sibling. That was my case- this is how I saw it growing up. I am considerably older than my brother. I was made to listen and do what was told. Adults always surrounded me- my parents, grandparents, and their friends for years. I was fine for the most part, but my dad and mother may have thought differently.

The second part of the verse: **"bring them up in discipline and instruction of the Lord,"** means it is the parents' job to make sure that they are involved in biblical teaching at home and in small peer groups like Sunday school and youth groups. We were brought up in the church, the Anglican church, and went to Sunday school every week. I loved it. I may have seen it as a social gathering, but it was always a time to learn bible verses and hear the bible readings each Sunday. Every Sunday, I went to church with my dad.

When my dad was the lay reader he would preach at the home for the mentally ill in Halifax. I would accompany him and play the organ, it was an old pump organ. During the first few visits, I was a little nervous. But later on, it became an excellent time for us to bond. I think we gained a real closeness.

When dad went to St. Timothy's church in Hatchett Lake, I also played the organ there. That made me feel I was raised according to the bible's teachings. And that is not to say we don't slip away from time to time in our lives. My dad and I reminisced about our times at the care home, me playing the organ and the residents sitting back enjoying the service. I always found the experience a little intimidating since the congregation was mentally ill and they would sit with their hands either folded on their laps or with them behind their heads and feet stretched out in front of them and stare at us. Still, they enjoyed the singing and the organ music. All the residents wore black runners with white laces and very plain clothes, almost like a uniform. I am sure it had to do with the budget.

We did the best we could with our girls. We brought them up in the church, and they both attended regularly. One went to bible college, and the other, at age 15, had enough of going to church. However, that was the end of it. A while ago the younger of the two, shared that we had made her go to church. I, as a parent, never saw it quite that way since my brother and I were expected to go every Sunday without fail. I watch how my children discipline their children and themselves. The children are molded in the way they feel is appropriate. We did the best we knew, and so did my parents. As far as the church, there were to be no excuses. I just did what was expected of me, no questions asked.

I went to Sunday school, girl's auxiliary, and Girl Guides. These were all at the church, St. Phillips, which now has a new name, the Anglican Church of the Apostles. I even took part in the junior choir. Most of my friends have the same routine of going to church, which made somewhat of a difference. Today many cultures and religious practices have evolved all over the world. I am not sure what happened, but I think it is best to let them go on their own and return at some point in their lives. You just need to plant the seeds.

Honor your father and mother Ephesians 6:2

In this verse, the apostle Paul is challenging us to teach our children to respect all authority so that they will become productive members of society as they grow. My dad and mom both instilled a work ethic into our lives. If our children learn to respect those who have authority, they will honor their teachers, coaches, bosses, and those who uphold the law. We also want to model respect with their peers and all people in general. Respect is a virtue that we need more of in today's culture, and instilling that in my children was extremely important to me. I believe I was fortunate to grow up where I had four adults leading me in the way of honor.

My grandfather played a big part, as did my father, in acquainting me to respect for others, and most of the time, it was by example.

The two male figures in my life, the most prominent ones, were respectful to their mother and father, and others. They were great role models for life.

Train up a child in the way he should go, and when he is old, he will not depart from it. Proverbs 22.6

Train up or dedicate your child in the way they should go. As parents, we are like shepherds who commit their children to the path our Heavenly Father has designed for them to follow. Our job was to dedicate our time to finding the way for our children—to help them find the purpose God had for their lives. We influenced this, but we were not in control of the outcome. Our job as shepherds and their fathers was to encourage our children to try different things to find what they enjoy and what fits within the plan that our Lord has for them as they grow. It may not be everyone's direction, but those with integrity and honesty could also lead their children.

I am not sure we followed the rules entirely, but we surely let them find their own way. It is imperative to let them follow their own path. In our world, as parents, we have spent most of our time taking them to after-school activities learning how to work with others so they would strive to be the best they could be.

My husband spent hours in our driveway playing basketball with my daughters and spent long hours showing them how to work around the house since we both worked out of the home. He also helped one of our daughters with music. Since she was a singer and played the piano, her dad would accompany her on his guitar. It is just one of the ways I try to live this verse. I pray for discernment every day for my children and their calling as they continue to move forward. In the same train of thoughts, my dad was supportive of all I did in school and the workplace, so I am thankful for this.

My parents had me in many after-school activities. I went to piano lessons by bus. We lived a fair distance from the Royal Conservatory of Music on Windsor Street and Connaught Avenue

Conversations with Dad

in Halifax.. I wasn't driven everywhere I needed to go. My mother didn't get her driver's license until I did. We both took lessons and got our licenses the same year, when I was 17. Dad had the task of teaching us both to drive, which is probably why his hair turned white at such a tender age. My parents taught me independence as well. Thank you, Dad.

Me: "Hey, Dad, do you remember when you taught mom and I to drive the car. Neither of us had our license, so you had the tremendous task of teaching us both. You had this amazing 1964 white meteor mercury with the back window that would roll down."

Dad: "How can I forget that time in our lives? I came home after a long day at the office and had supper and then took your mother out for the driving experience. And after about half an hour or so, you would be sitting there waiting for your turn when I returned. I was exhausted some days. Your mother took her test and had no problem. On the other hand, you left classes one morning for the test, and the examiner was Harold Mayes, a friend of ours. You were very nervous, but I was confident you would do alright and pass the test. Well, I was wrong. You came back in tears. I forgot to teach you how to parallel park. Harold gave me a lecture about not teaching you how to parallel park."

Me: "I had to return to classes and tell everyone I didn't pass the test. Oh, it was alright. I survived the ordeal and booked another appointment and, of course, passed the test. Poor you, dad, you never had your car again. Well, that was remedied. You bought mom a Valiant automatic car. I got to use it once in a while. It was the one with the push-button gear shift exchange. So Cool."

Dad chuckled.

Me: "Dad, did I ever tell you what happened to that car one night I took it to work at Dominions Stores on the Golden Mile?"

Dad: "Oh no, what happened?"

Me: "I think it is alright to tell you now that I am an adult and you are a senior citizen. You won't get mad at me, right. But not sure you would have blown a gasket, although I am sure my gentile mother would have. This is how it went. After work at the grocery store (Dominion Stores), we all went to Reid's Diner, up the hill from there. (It is a Tim Horton's now). We were at least 10 friends—all high school students. We ordered milkshakes and junk food and laughed and joked about work and our lives. It was almost midnight, so we all had to go home, and some had to return to the store in the morning.

We went out to the parking lot. I was about to get into mom's car. Mmm, the car was gone.!! It was gone!! Oh my gosh. I was slightly concerned, and I am sure she would have been too. So, I thought, where is it. I have always been contemplative in stressful situations, which maybe is your influence. I ventured out of the parking lot and looked over at the grocery store, and it was parked there. I was sure I had driven it up to the Diner. What had happened? A few of the guys were playing a gag on me and had rolled it down the hill. When I found out, I was shocked but didn't bust a gut or say much, just hopped in the car and came back home. I had never told either one of you. I did tell mom a few years ago."

Dad: "That was a pretty good story. Did that really happen?"
Me: "Yes, it did!!"
Dad: (smiled ear to ear) "Is there anything else you have not told me?"
Me: "no, that is all for now."
So here unfolds the story of my relationship with my dad.

My dad's mother and father and his oldest sister Margaret.

CHAPTER 3

Life without Mother

I always enjoyed chatting with Dad.

When he tells me his old stories, my heart and brain travel backward in time with him, and his experiences become my experiences. And for that, I have always been and still am most grateful.

Who is my daddy, then? It's hard to know where to start, but I guess I'll begin with my mother's death, the most critical and most devastating event in his life to date.

Mom passed away in 2019, and Dad has had a terrible time ever since; that obviously makes sense.

They were married for almost 72 years. Since my mom's death, there hasn't been a day he hasn't spent time thinking about her.

Her photo still hangs above the TV. The light above the Television highlights my mother's picture. She is sitting in Taberna de las Flores, a restaurant in Colmenar, Spain. It was Christmas 2011. We walked from our daughter's home to the restaurant. In the picture, Mom has that wry grin on her face that she often had. She looks very content and happy to have her family around. She didn't always speak too much, so she spent a lot of time taking in and living the moment. I am sure that is why dad gets such joy from this photo. She is sitting at a table with two candles and a glass of white wine. This Christmas gathering at Taberna Flores was a group from the language school where Frank (my husband) took Spanish lessons, so we were all invited.

Dad arranged for us all to go to Spain for Christmas that year. That was incredibly generous of him. We were all there except for Jessica and her family, who lived in India at the time. We had a wonderful Christmas. My mom, dad, and I reached first in Spain a few days before my brother and his two children.

The tradition for Christmas dinner in Spain is not a turkey dinner. Most Spanish Christmas dinners are with roast goat or langoustines(prawns). We were looking for a place where we could order a turkey since we wanted somewhat of a traditional Christmas as well as the Spanish traditions too. There was a butcher shop on the same street as our daughter's, from where we were able to order a turkey.

We bought an artificial tree and made it like our festival in Canada since our other relatives wanted to celebrate the traditional Christmas they do in Canada. There were not many Christmas trees in Spain; in fact, I don't think I have ever seen any. We bought a live tree and put it on the rooftop garden after Christmas one year.

My parents were such great sports. They were both fit and well into their 80s and played alongwith us whatever we chose to do. They both took turns; on one of the days, my dad went with my brother and his children to Gibraltar while my mom stayed with Karen, Isis, and me. On another day, my brother and his two children, along with Frank and me, went to El Torcal, a nature reserve in the Sierra del Torcal Mountain range located south of the city of Antequera, in the province of Malaga. It is known for its unusual landforms and is regarded as one of the most impressive landscapes in Europe. The area was designated as a natural site of national interest in July 1929. A natural park reserve of about 17 square kilometers was then created in October 1978.

My dad was generous by nature. On their 60th wedding

anniversary, he took the entire family on an Alaskan cruise. My daughters did not come since one lived in India and the other in Spain.

There was only one guideline for the trip we could do which kept us pleased all day, but we had to be back for dinner in the dining room for the family to eat together. Mom, Dad, Frank, and I went on a few tours together, and the other foursome did their own thing. We went to a pioneer town where there was gold panning. This indeed shows family is vital to him. We were able to keep this policy for him. So, we used to dress for the dining room each evening and sit for dinner, the eight of us. Once dinner was over, the kids went off on their own to join the other teenagers on board, and the remaining six went to see the evening show.

Most days, dad sits in his captain's chair watching TV and looks up at my mom's photo from time to time. If anyone dares turn the TV off, he makes a serious effort to turn it back on. There's also a picture of my mom hanging in the bedroom- a copy of my friend Sandy's painting for me. Of course, it's been hard for all of us. My dad often sweetly says, "I know you two (me and my brother) are missing her too."

There was always one exciting thing when we were young. Dad used to take me shopping at Christmas to get mom her gift. We bought some lovely dresses for her and jewelry too. He was very generous with gifts for mom. I was always hoping my life partner would be a romantic as well. Not everyone is as romantic as my dad. I used to stand back and watch him charm the ladies at the Hudson Bay jewelry department. It was so natural for him. The ladies grinned from ear to ear and would be attentive when waiting for him.

Another lovely thing Dad used to do is as we used to be away 3 out of 4 weeks a month. He always bought my mom home some YARDLEY SOAP products. Mom always had lavender soap and powder as well. That was so romantic of my dad. He so loved our mom.

I am sure it is much harder for dad since they were together all the time in the last five years of my mom's life. Mom did not let him go anywhere on his own. They were a very close couple. If one of them needed a nap or laydown the other would also lap down as well. That is love. They had a special bond. They went everywhere together too. Indeed, a married couple's love differs from a child's and parents. After so many years, I find myself and my husband going everywhere too, but that truly does not match their kind of love.

This is me on the car, my dad, my mom and grandmother, family was everything to my dad. Waiting for the ferry to Prince Edward Island.

CHAPTER 4

His strength and High energy

From time to time, Dad still asks me, "You have no complaints about your childhood, do you?"

My answer comes effortlessly every time he asks, "Dad! I had a wonderful childhood, and I have so many great memories. I say that with honesty and sincerity. There is nothing I ever wanted for and never went without. We weren't rich and famous, but you were always a good provider, Dad.

Me: How about you dad and your growing up years?

Dad: Well, I had a pretty good life. I was treated very well by both my parents. I loved them both, but I think I may have been closer to my mom than my dad. On Friday nights, the entire family would walk about a 2.1 km distance from Chebacco Rd. to downtown to Gottingen Street shopping. The men doodled along while the women did the shopping. Dad would buy us an ice cream cone, and if he saw something little we liked, he would give us the money to buy it. Dad would never deny us anything. It was the entire family, including dear ole granny.

Me: We were upper-middle class. I feel rich in many ways. We always had a lovely house and a spacious backyard. We regularly went on summer holiday trips, often with my grandparents. Dad loves to tell the story of how my grandfather would ask my dad when his holidays were going to take place, and then he would book his at the same time. So, the six of us quite often enjoyed holidays together.

 I love my dad. He is still a prominent imposing figure, although he used to be much taller than he is now. He is in his nineties. As we age, we lose space between the discs in our spine, the arachnoid case. So, my dad has shrunk quite a lot. When I first realized his towering height, he was about 6'2" tall, and now he is only 5'11". I will soon tower over my dad. I am only 5' 9 1/2"

 My dad is fortunate in many ways. He got a wake-up call when he was about 45. He nearly had a heart attack and was put on a strict diet and exercise regime by his heart doctor. As far as arthritis goes, he is virtually pain-free, something many seniors have to deal with because of poor nutrition. He had open-heart surgery on 9/11,2001 due to the hardening of arteries and had a good recovery. He had his appendix removed in 1960, which is all he has had.

 He takes excellent care of what he eats, even in his late 90s. A short while ago, he had minor non-invasive surgery and recovered well. He fell while departing from Denny's on a Saturday morning and broke his left humerus in three places. It was his most debilitating downfall; he had no cast, though, just immobilized with a brace.

 About seven years ago, when my parents moved from their townhouse to the condo, they did quite a lot of the packing. Frank and I, did the lion's share of the packing as it was a big job. It was difficult for the both of them to let go of some precious things. But the two of them (mom and dad) were amid the packing, and they didn't miss a beat.

 I was always in awe of my dad. I looked up to him not just because he was so tall and so big and I was so small and so short, but now that was when I was a little girl. He has such a loud, forceful voice. I didn't realize I had such a booming voice until I was chatting on the phone with Dad one evening. He was on speaker phone mode, and apparently, I was also talking very loudly. Our house

Conversations with Dad

guest came barreling upstairs thinking there was an intruder because of the loud voices. I was always afraid to ask him a question. He was away most of my childhood, so it was a grand celebration whenever he came home on weekends. He usually brought some gifts or tokens for mom and me, and then when my brother was in the picture, I suppose he got something too.

I remember coming home from school for lunch one day from Westmount Elementary. I was in Grade 8, and we had just gotten the results of our end-of-year marks.

Dad asked, "Did you pass?"

I replied, "oh, dad, I didn't do all well. "(which was a total lie).

He was a little puzzled. I had always got on the honor roll. So, we finished lunch, and I headed back. By the time I returned to school, Mrs. Christie had received a phone call from dad asking why I hadn't done all that well. She confronted me and asked why I told him that? I thought it was a funny way of playing a joke on him. He wasn't impressed or mad, nor was Mrs. Christie. That was my mom who scolded me.

He says he still has a good sense of humor. My dad always played jokes on us, and I thought this was my opportunity. It didn't go well.

You may ask yourselves why I write a story about my dad. Well, it is because I want others to know who he is. I feel we need to celebrate our parents. I want to honor my dad. I just want everyone to know he lived a great life and one to be proud of and honored.

My Dad and me stopped at Hope for wildlife refuge near Dartmouth Nova Scotia.

CHAPTER 5

Remembering Ole Granny. And trips to Boston

I remember my grandmother trusted my dad right from the beginning. Dad told me when he had asked my mother to marry him, and she first said, "Tom, you will have to ask my parents first."

Later, he was introduced to her grandparents, who lived in Jordan Ferry near Shelburne, Nova Scotia. My dad didn't have a car, so my grandmother went to ask Oscar (my grandfather) for the key to his car and gave the keys to my dad to drive to Jordan Ferry to meet mom's grandparents.

Me: "How was it? Your relationship was so fantastic with your mom? I had a great mom as well. I think you knew. Tee hee. Were you as close with your mom as I was with my mom?"

Dad: "I had a fantastic mother. I caused problems, but whose kids don't? In grade 10, I was sent to a private school in Church Point, Nova Scotia, about 30 km south of Digby. The Eudist Fathers ran it."

Me: "Hey, dad, I never caused problems" (wink wink.)

Me: "Dad, what was it like growing up in your household? You know what it was like in our house. Can you tell me what it was like for you?"

Dad: "My parents were so good to me. I never wanted for anything. I was the only boy, and my mom once said, "Tommy, if you had been born first, there would not have been any more children."

"I always felt that was a bit of a roque statement for a mother to say to her young son. (He probably was taken aback a little when he said this to me) Dad: As you know, I had two sisters who were older than me, so when I arrived on the scene, it was a pretty special event. If you get my drift, a boy is definitely revered in a family."

Me: "My recollection of this similar hierarchy of a male presence makes me think of a co-worker I had working in a clinic many years ago. She was pregnant with her first child, and there was great excitement for her and all of us. Mary Ellen was a typical subservient wife, yes dear, no dear, and nothing much. Some offices required the pregnant party to resign from their jobs at six months of pregnancy time in those old times. So, we had a shower for Mary Ellen. She left us, and about three months later, we heard she and her husband became parents of a baby girl. The husband was devastated and very disappointed. The couple stayed together for about a year, and then he left her since she could not deliver a male child. That was so like Henry VII. We all know that the male is the deciding factor."

My husband and I had been asked several times after we had two daughters. "Are you going to try again for a boy?"

I never quite understood the boldness of the individuals who asked such a thing.

I looked shocked and responded, "I don't need a boy. We will maybe get a boy if our daughters marry one day."

My dad's family was proud of their son, and of course, they should have been just as proud of their daughters. That may have just been their way of saying how proud they were of Tommy- my dad. They should have been just as proud of their daughters too. Right?

Some cultures still today revere the male more than the female child but it is cultural.

Dad: "In our household, there were four women in the family- Mom, two sisters, and grandma, who immigrated to Canada after her husband had left her a widow. So, the men, your grandfather, who was my dad, and I were overpowered by the estrogen levels. One outlandish thing I remember about my grandmother is that she warned us in her gruff voice. if you leave toys around for others to trip over, she would boldly say," If I step over them again, I put them in the fire." I thought that that was horrible, but that was ole granny Horrick."

My grandmother was harsh, but we loved her, especially when she would hug us into her bosom, and the sweet smell of mothballs will remain ever in my mind.

I must tell you about the time Granny Herrick died. I think she had a heart attack, and when she was to be laid out for viewing, she was placed in our parlor, and the top was left open, of course. We- Mary and I, Mary was my best friend, sneaked in after everyone was gone, touched Granny's wrinkled hands, and kissed her on her forehead. We were about nine years old at the time. We were not afraid of her anymore. She could no longer throw our possession into the fire; that was her threat for not picking up our stuff. We still loved ole Granny.

Dad tells of being taken on trips to Boston with his parents and sometimes just with his mother. He speaks very lovingly of his relationship with his parents and is very proud of his mother's accomplishments. She was touted as the primary breadwinner in the family. It seemed she was the boss or the captain of the ship.

Not that my grandfather didn't work quite the contrary. He not only worked full time after returning from the war overseas, but he received a pension, so the family was financially alright. Dad says his father received his money earned in a little brown envelope on payday and gave it to his mother. She would, in turn, give him $ 2.00 in spending money. He says his dad always had money. He didn't spend much he would buy the kids an ice cream once in a while or a treat or buy himself a cigar. I believe those who survived the depression have that mindset that they didn't have much, even if they did have enough.

Dad: "There was one trip my mother and dad took to Boston on their own, and they brought me back a lovely leather school bag, one you could either wear on your back or with a handle. I loved that bag, but the kids were so mean and mocked me for carrying such a bag. I am sure they were just plain jealous. I didn't care for a time as it was a great school bag. Jealousy is horrible!"

Dad: "My mother cleaned and redecorated the house every spring. Painted all the walls and sometimes repair the home. She did this process where she dabbed a sponge on the entire walls on top of the freshly painted walls in contrasting colors. She was a hard worker, for sure."

Me: "Dad, do you remember the great times we had going to Boston and visiting with the Detorre family? Those were some of my best holiday memories. When we were young, on vacation, we would see our cousins. We call them our cousins, but only kissing cousins but they are like family to us. We loved staying at their house. It was so big and exciting with so many curio cupboards and China cabinets. One is filled with salt and pepper shakers. There must be over 200 sets. I had never seen so many. They were all still there when we visited about five years ago. I recently chatted with my cousin Lea, and she said they are in the process of reorganizing the present house, and the next time we visit, they may have already moved."

I told my dad about the pending sale of the house, and he said," oh, I would love to own that house." That house is such a legacy to that family and our family.

There was a lot of property attached to that house, so we played in the woods and just had great fun. On my last visit as a teenager, I remember my cousin Kathy was working at the dairy queen. Oh, that was great because she brought home boxes of dilly bars and ice cream sandwiches. And best of all was the chicken cacciatore. It was Uncle Freddie that made this dish. He was a repairman for freezers and air conditioners. He worked many night shifts. When he got home from work, he used to sit in the easy chair and watch American baseball. But his specialty food was, of course, his chicken cacciatore. Even in the last few visits, we flew to Boston with the entire gang, including dad, mom Sherry, Nigel, Frank, and me; that was so much fun. The highlight of the trip as far as sightseeing goes was the city of Boston tour on the Duck Boat. I don't know whether or not those reading this know what a duck boat is, but I will attempt to explain. A duck boat will often be a refurbished DUKW vehicle built by General Motors and used extensively in World War II.

With the passing of Aunt Catherine (she was only called aunt out of respect). We hear from the offspring from time to time, they are my generation. The place will not be the same. I used to love listening to her in conversation. What a beautiful accent. Dad gets quite nostalgic when we talk about Boston and then tells me the story of his honeymoon.

Dad: "Yes, I remember meeting Katherine for the first time when they went on honeymoon and me and your mom stayed back to visit for few more days. Freddie and Katherine started out for Florida on their honeymoon but changed their mind and only went as far as New York City and returned home early. that is what we found out later. It was a hilarious incident. Your mom and I were just getting settled into our hotel in Boston when a knock at the door. Who could that be? We both gasped! We didn't really know anyone here except the kissing cousins, and we hadn't met them yet. Upon opening the door, it was Katherine's sister Jean. Neither of us had met her, and she said in her very assertive manner. "Pack your bags. You are staying at the house in Bellingham." We had no choice but to go. Cousin Jean checked us out of the hotel and we were off to the big house.

So, it was planned that we would go to the wedding but from the hotel. We traveled by Greyhound Bus from Halifax to Boston after our wedding reception a few days later. I didn›t have my car at this time. Oh, Susan, I remember the wedding cakes. One was the traditional three-layer fruit cake at this wedding, and the other was an ice cream cake.

Someone had forgotten to take it out of the freezer, and they had to get an electric tool to cut the darn thing. We had such a great time at this wedding. When the wedding was done, and Katherine and Freddy left on the honeymoon, we stayed on for a few more days of our honeymoon and then headed back to Halifax, so I could find a job. We traveled back by way of a Greyhound bus."

Dad always says that mom got him the job at Pilkington Glass. She had written a reply to an advertisement she had noticed in the Halifax Chronicle Herald.

Dad: "She hadn't told me she wrote the letter at first. It wasn't until I received a phone call for an interview. Your mother was constantly surprising me with something. We did so many crazy things together."

He was such an exceptional sales agent for Pilkington Glass. Dad tells me quite often how that is the only thing he ever wanted to do in life. SELL! And he sold a lot of different products, but the glass was his last hurrah. Well, that isn't entirely true. After retirement, my mother had a dream to have a teddy bear store, so being a wonderful man, husband, and father, he obliged my momma, and we all contributed to the project. He was the main person in the shop every day since we all had other jobs. I was a nurse, my brother was also in sales, my husband was a health care provider, and my mom was a sales associate at the former Woodward's department store. So, it was dad in the store selling teddy bears and party supplies and balloon bouquets. There is definite evidence a salesman was his plight in life.

Dad taking a break from reading having a coffee.
He loves his Coffee.

CHAPTER 6

Vacations with my family

I was very fortunate to grow up with the parents like mine. They both came from British routes and were from similar backgrounds in some tracks. Life was so good growing up with my mom, dad, and grandparents. The age difference between my younger brother and me was almost eight years, and my dad never lets me forget I am older. We lived at the bottom of the street, and the grandparents lived at the top.

Many times I would travel with my dad alone to Prince Edward Island. I stayed with our very good friends, the Birts. We are still friends to this day.

Mom, dad and I, usually went camping, in a tent with no floor. Three trips come to mind when remembering camping trips, in particular. There was the one when I was about 6, and we were on our way to Bangor, Maine. We were traveling from Halifax, where we lived at the time. We stopped at this campground as far as St. George, New Brunswick. We had supper cooked on the ole Coleman stove, probably beans, and wieners, but that is a long time ago to remember what was on the menu of the day.

We sat around the campfire and chatted. I went to bed in this lovely large white canvas tent with no bottom. All modern tents have the floor, and if there is no bottom, one usually digs a trench. We didn't put a trench around the perimeter of the tent. We were fast asleep, and for some unknown reason, dad woke up.

He shouted, "Hey, you two, we are floating."

I can still remember this as if it was just yesterday. The rain was torrential, and we were floating on our air mattresses. At that moment, dad says, "We should have trenched around the tent. Hindsight is always drier!!"

We quickly got up, folded our bags, stuffed everything in dad's car trunk, and headed for the nearest motel. That is one vacation I will never forget.

My dad talks about the other vacation when the six of us, including my grandparents, went camping in our old tent trailer. It was new when we bought it. It was a good tent trailer, but someone forgot to lock the back legs of the box. While dad, granddad, and my brother were off getting donuts for all of us, my mother and grandmother experienced the trailer collapse on one end. There was great screaming and gnashing of teeth. They were so freaked out and I somehow got on board with the drama. We were all dressed to go to church, resulting in the finest clothes we could bring on a camping trip.

When the men returned, the women and (somehow, I always get included) tore a strip off two men. I felt sorry for them. I am thinking now it had nothing to do with them being so long away but the fact that the tent trailer had collapsed. Not sure if we ever used it again. I can still hear the screams in the memory bank of my mind.

The third camping trip was with my grandparents again. My brother and I called them GranGran and Mum even into our thirties when they passed away. They were with us most vacations, and they were such great sports. We slept in a Coleman brand tent this particular year known as a Tourist tent, but this was a classic design. The back of the tent has a jut-out back, which allows for two more people and a double air mattress. My grandparents slept there. We were on our way back from a family trip to Boston and stopped for the night in Ellsworth, Maine- a lovely campsite. It was warm and dry when we went to bed. Everyone was fast asleep. The word fast is a derivative of the Old German word fest, which means "stuck firmly or strongly; not easily movable." So, to be fast asleep is to be immovable or permanently sleeping.

Suddenly, out of the dark, a voice echoed; my grandmother's chirping voice, "Tom, Tom, Oscar, and I are all wet."

This is another family photo taken at Peggy's Cove. Nova Scotia.

What happened was a considerable leak in the seam of the roof of their section. My grandparents were swimming in sleeping bags, but the rest of us were high and dry. We quickly got everyone up. It was early enough that we could get up and pack up and head for the dry country in the morning. We laughed and cried. These grandparents were so flexible that they didn't complain. They didn't call my dad out for help in the night. He was their hero. They were calling the name of their hero.

There was another short trip with my dad. I had actually gone with my school friend Catherine Russell to her summer cottage. It was near Pictou, Nova Scotia. We always had good times either at her house or mine. My dad was on his return trip from Prince Edward Island, and he was to drop by the summer place and pick me up to return home. That was all well and good. I had woven a pretty good yarn while with Catherine and her brother George.

I concocted a story about my dad and our family and that I was born in Japan while dad was a missionary there, and when he returned, he got into sales with his present company at the time Pilkington Glass. It was such a great story the only diversion was George came on the return ride to Halifax.

We enjoyed our ride home. George was in the back seat and started grilling my dad about his experiences in Japan. Oopsy!! I was busted. We all laughed about it, but later, dad said to me, "you should have given me a heads up. I would have backed up the story." I'm glad I was busted. It would have carried on too long, and it wasn't true, just me trying to tell stories like my dad.

Mom Frank Dad in Alaska, there he is with a book in his hand.

Dad was always very involved in his work, and when he was home, he got involved in the church. He speaks of how he helped

Conversations with Dad

build the church, St. Phillips Anglican. He was very proud of his involvement. He tells of the original building of St. Phillips was an army hut on the grounds of Westmount School. It was dismantled after the new church was built.

My parents were very social. They made up for absent time away from each other. Dad was organizing many churches' social activities. He was into the square dancing and the bowling league, and curling. There were always so many people at our house. Dad and I have reminisced a lot over the last few years. It was dad's third Christmas since mom's passed, I decided to leave Spain and return to Canada to Langley to check on my dad. My daughter and husband stayed with him as he likes having someone around. During our last week, we spent a lot of time chatting and going for coffee at his favorite nearby haunt, Denny's. Dad loves to venture across the street and go to Denny's and enjoys the staff hovering over him. It is like "Cheers," where everyone knows his name, and they bring him his coffee and his usual breakfast as soon as he sits down. He tells me this every time we chat.

The last evening before heading back to Spain to rejoin my husband and granddaughter, he and I were alone, and I cooked a supper he loves; Macaroni and cheese, his favorite with veggies. After supper, we just continued our reminiscing, and then we started to do what mom always asked me to do when we needed to know the answer to some unknown; "Susan, Look it up on Google."

Karen Mom Isis Dad and Me.

So, we looked up many things, watched animal videos on YouTube, and had a lot of great discussions. We tend to do that. I will miss him when I am back in my own house. He promised he would come to visit me in the spring. He is and will always be most welcome in our house. My parents dropped in unannounced many times over the years, for a meal or just for a coffee. We had an open-door policy.

CHAPTER 7

Road trip across Canada

After mom passed away, we stayed on the west coast for another year and decided we would return to our home on the east coast. We rented our house to a local person and had only planned to stay for three months and then return. Six years later, we did manage to collect more stuff, and we couldn't part with it all. We had rented a cargo trailer to haul behind our new SUV, packed it to the gunnels, and even packed the dog and Dad. They were in the SUV, not the cargo trailer. After much deliberation, he agreed to come along. There were a few hitches, of course. My brother's family didn't like the idea of us kidnapping dad; how could he possibly survive a trip across the country. In the beginning, the plan was to visit for a few days with Rick and Ilze then they would take dad to the airport. He was to fly to Montreal, where we would meet him, and travel from there to New Brunswick.

O the day of departure and at the very last minute, he changed his mind. He packed his bags and even his medications for two months were inside. The plan was averted- he changed his mind and wasn't coming, so the three of us, Frank, Dad, and I went across the street for breakfast anyway. After Breakfast we hugged dad and said goodbye and left. He was changing his mind every ten seconds.

That's not the end of our departure experience. We headed east on the number one highway, and we were almost to Hope about 100 km away when my cell phone rang.

A voice on the other end said, "Hi, where are you?" it was my dad. He had finished breakfast, and dear sweet Nicholas (my nephew) had dropped his grandpa off at his Condo.

Dad: "I want to go with you. Would you come back and get me?"
Me: "Of course, dad. We are on our way!"

When we returned, he was out front with his suitcase saying goodbye to one of the Ladies from his condo building, and at the same time, he fell because he was hugging her. She was quite a lot shorter than him. So, dad got into the car, and we headed back to Highway Number one to Edmonton. The story doesn't end there.

We made it to Blue River and stayed there the first night, and when we awoke, dad said, "I don't have my pills."

It was my judgmental error. As I reflect, I probably would have been best to go back and check if anything was missing from dad's suitcase. So, we go into recovery mode. We went to the next town, Valemont, where there is a pharmacy, and had the pharmacist contact. We had to wait around for another few hours to get it sorted. They gave us a 10-day supply to get us across the country and then we headed to Edmonton. We contacted our dearest friend Sandy, and she got the blister pack of pills and sent them to us in New Brunswick. We did good brainstorming.

We had a great trip. Dad is someone who loves to eat out, so this trip was his Valhalla. He ate every meal out across Canada. While we waited for Rita to continue with us, we did some drives down memory lane. We drove by our old house on 42 avenues, and Frank and I went to the church we were married in, St. John's Anglican, to see how it had changed. Edmonton certainly has changed since we left over 30 years ago.

Dad loves to repeat this statement; "Do you know what your mother always said when I asked her what we should have for lunch or dinner? She always said "reservations" for dinner."

There were some days they ate all three meals out. I recall one day, after returning from work and I asked what they had for supper. Just out of curiosity of course.

Mom: "We went to White Spot."
Me: "Oh, that is great. What about lunch?"
Mom: "Oh, we went to Wendall's in Fort Langley."
Me: "Oh, at least you had one meal at home."
Mom: "Well, no." After much deliberation, she sheepishly replied, "We ate at Denny's."

I hooted. That was not always, but at least two meals were out on some days. They were such a sweet couple. They loved to share a meal. Stamp-out home cooking was her motto! Dad finds a whole meal too much. He has a close firend now who will sometimes share a meal with him otherwise he brings home the other half and it sits in the fridge with the others from previous meals out.

Back to the stopover in Edmonton, it was great. We had previously arranged to stop for a few days with Rick and Ilze while we waited for Rita to be ready to continue with us. We had prearranged to do a caravan with her across the country. She had her life possessions shipped, and in the car were her two dogs and 18-year-old cat.

Dad is so easy to get so long as there is coffee involved, and there is always coffee when my dad is there. Rick and Ilze treated us like real guests and even gave up their own beds. Dad had a captive audience to tell his stories. He has many great stories. Some of which I will share as the book continues.

As the trip progressed, we only stopped and visited with one other friend, and that was in northern Manitoba. My friend lives in the Moosehorn area, and we stayed in Ashern. The only place to stay was a sketchy hotel attached to a pub. Many people lived there full-time, and the rooms were alright. Both Rita and I put blankets on top of the bed linen and did not move all night, thinking the bedbugs would attack us or the neighbors would break into our place. There was quite a commotion when we arrived at midnight. From our visit to Moosehorn area. That was us at first, then a few of the neighbors started yelling keep the noise down, and a few got up and tossed empty bottles out the door. The next closest place was about 100km away, so we sucked it up and made it through the night.

I think this was quite an adventure to go north from Dauphin. Thanks to Erica and Jim for a lovely visit.

Mom Dad Me Jordan Ferry Nova Scotia.

CHAPTER 8

Pandemic and Isolation

It was still pandemic - Covid 19. There was an initial two weeks when Dad had to stay since it was during the pandemic, so we all had to isolate ourselves. It was easy to isolate at our place. We live on a small acreage so that we could wander on the property. We have made many generous and amazing friends in New Brunswick. To mention only a few, like Lana and her family, who brought us some groceries while we were in isolation. Heather also brought us some groceries. Tammy, our next-door neighbor, picked up food from the Super Store. So many people in Salisbury (the town closest to us) have been great. One even got us a bottle of white wine; how decadent, and we are Baptists. Another friend Lew came late at night with some spray to kill the wasps that were circling the house. I can't say enough good things about the friends we have made here in New Brunswick.

The first part of the journey was here in my front yard. I had a tablespoon of mom's ashes that I placed under a forsythia tree in my front garden. It was mom's favorite shrub she had planted in a couple of the yards of houses she lived in. We had traveled around the province a little, and the plan was to take some of mom's ashes to her grandparents' grave in Jordan Ferry, Nova Scotia. Before the trip, we had even arranged to have mom's name and years engraved on the back of the same headstone as her grandparents.

Frank, I, and dad managed to locate the actual gravestone in the cemetery in Jordan Ferry. It was quite an emotional afternoon. We arrived with no utensils or tools to dig the ground in front of the gravestone, so we improvised the stick we found in the woods near the cemetery. We dug into the grass and poured mom's ashes. We each said some kind words after we managed to deposit her ashes at the grave site. It was our private memorial.

Dad was quite tearful. Later we drove into the town of Shelburne to find a florist and ended up at the local nursery-Spencer's Garden center and nursery. They sold something called a saddle, which straddled the tombstones in cemeteries. We purchased one for mom's grave site and placed it on the gravestone. Dad was extremely pleased with what we had done for his beautiful bride.

He said he had to return home to British Columbia since that is where mom, her spirit, and everything was. I understood. We made arrangements for my brother to meet him in Toronto with his son. We drove him to Halifax airport. He flew with the family from Toronto to Vancouver. I was sad to see him go, but I had to honor his wishes at this time. While we were waiting for his flight, I had an opportunity; it may not have been the best time, but why not ask now?

All my life, I wondered why we had never had a relationship with dad's parents-our grandparents. We had spoken of this topic several times, but it was always taboo and washed over. I never had an explanation, so I left it alone until years later when my dad left Moncton to return to his home in Langley. I asked him why it was that way? And he started to tell me various scenarios.

He just said in the end, "I don't really know why my family never got along with your mother's family." after this being said, I decided to just to drop it. It may unnecessarily drag up a lot of pain for a man in his nineties. I always felt horrible about mentioning this to him since what could he do about this situation. Everyone had passed away except his two nephews and their families, estranged from dad. And the rest of us, for that matter.

Me: «It is a fact I do not get along with my brother. I don›t know why. I have tried to pass him an olive branch a few times, but he has refused. He said to me once when I offered to go to counseling with him, « oh, you can›t get along with everyone.» I was going to even to pay for the shot. I pray it will be better; that is all one can do. How was your relationship with your sisters?"

Dad: I had two sisters older than me. I got along for the most part with them. But I am sure they thought I was a nuisance most of the time since I was always tagging along with them. My mother would bellow from the kitchen, since she spent most of her time there, «Margaret and Gracie, please take your little brother with you.» It was most of the time until I was old enough to play with my own friends. I am sure they were glad to be free from me as a tag-along. I had one favorite friend that was Brad Matthews. He didn›t live close, about 4 or 5 blocks from our house. But we went to the same school. He was as naughty as I was. After playing, I would always come home dirty and covered in dust and dirt. Mother would send me to take a bath every time I came home from playing with my friends.

Oh, I had another friend Mary Campbell and have always wondered what had happened to her. I lost contact. She was also friends with my two older sisters.

We only had two bikes, so the three siblings had to share. So, whoever got there first; got the bike. It was always a race between Gracie and me to get the bike. Margaret always got a bike as she was older and bossy. She and I didn't get along. Gracie and I were closer than Margaret and I. I don't know why; that is just how it was. Margaret was a little offish with most people and spent most of her off time with Mom."

We had an unfortunate altercation which was averted by my husband several years ago when we went to a nursing home in Mississauga, Ontario, where my dad's sister Margaret was residing.

She was in the end stages of dementia. Her younger son got wind of us having visited the home two days previous, and he wanted to be there if we came for another visit. We were in the lobby, and the nephew came charging at dad. We were all quite shocked at this behavior. Frank stepped in and prevented John from delivering a sucker punch to my dad's head. He didn't think Dad had any right to see his mother. He accused my dad of being the problem with his family. We had no idea what it was all about. The four of us left immediately and returned to the home of the other brother Lawrence who also got wind of the visit and was very angry with us for visiting his mother. We never heard from them, Lawrence and June, until my dad's other sister Grace passed away. That has been almost 20 years now, and we still have nothing no information about the schism. We will never know. Some things are best left buried.

Another trip we made was when dad was here with us trying to locate his parent's home in Enfield, Nova Scotia. We did not find it, but I have seen a picture of it since then and will find it one day.

Me: dad, why did we never have any relationship with your parents? Our other grandparents?

Dad: I really don't know what to say to you. I wish they had gotten to know you, but it just wasn't meant to be.

We hugged and looked at each other with some perplexity and said goodbye.

It was always a great mystery why we never got to know our paternal grandparents. Both my brother and I had never been to their home in Halifax or when they moved to Enfield- a small hamlet outside Halifax. It is near the international airport.

Enfield is a small urban community located 5 kilometers or 3.1 miles from the Halifax Stanfield International Airport in the Shubenacadie Valley in Hants County and Halifax counties in Nova Scotia, Canada.

Dad and I had some great conversations about events of his growing up and when my brother and I were kids. I got to know my dad more after my mom's death. He started to share a lot of his past.

Conversations with Dad

My dad visited his mother on his way home from work on Fridays, which I never knew as a young child. He only told us a few years ago. When his mother died, I recall him going to a funeral, and he told us years later that the staff at his office, Pilkington Glass, were the pallbearers for his mother. Dad's family was very private, so they didn't know many to ask for help as pallbearers. Thus, they had very few friends to call upon for funeral services.

Once my parents and I were at their home in Enfield but did not stay. We just dropped by for a few minutes, and I saw my grandfather on the stairs. I never met him again. I remember I was so young.

Then there was another time we saw my grandmother Taylor when she was shopping at the Halifax Shopping Centre years later with my cousin Lawrence and his mother (my aunt Margaret). They didn't stop, I knew they had seen us, but my mother casually pointed out who they were. My paternal grandfather had passed away already.

We all have issues, and we don't know what they are. We need to be mindful of others' feelings, but having said that very profound statement, I still wonder what it was all about, and we will never know now.

I have the mind of an uncanny detective. I will ask my cousin Lawrence what it was all about. I tried to contact him twice on telephone tag.

I never met him either until he was getting married, and that was when he was well into his forties. He is about six years older than me since my mom had said he was four years old at their wedding. I was born about two years later, so six years is the difference in my calculation. So, we knew very little about the family.

My mother never spoke of them much, yet my grandmother Sedman said she always thought it strange that they didn't get along either. She said there had been words exchanged over the years. Grandmother Sedman always said they were very nasty to my mother, and I would never comprehend why? My mother was so sweet and would not hurt a flea. Grandma once said that my parents were invited for dinner at my mom's in-law's place after my parent's marriage. They made snide remarks about how little food my mother would consume and how thin she was. She was brought tears on one occasion and did not like revisiting them.

Dad with his Sister Grace

CHAPTER 9

Paris trip with the Kiwanis.

Every time Dad moved cities; he would get involved in the Kiwanis club. I think he has fond memories kindled around the events with the Kiwanis club. As a very young girl, I remember going to a meeting with my dad at the Nova Scotia hotel. It was an evening with just the men and the children. I can still remember my dress. It was a blue satin dress, and I looked so lovely. That is my recollection, but I think my dad thought the same too. He was always so proud of me.

Then there was the time the club was selling peppermint patties, and he came home with a full trunk. He loves this memory. His car smelled of peppermint for a year, at least. We all helped him sell the patties too. All my friends from the church group helped. Dad gave us all a free pass for the movie theatre.

When he lived in White Rock, the club went on a trip to Europe, a lifetime journey for them. Many of the people who did go were not Kiwanians, just dad and mom's friends. They were great for attracting others to have fun.

It reminds me of when mom and dad casually asked Doris and her friend Shirley, "Would you like to come to England with us?"

And of course, they said yes. It became a bit of a trip where mom and dad were the caretakers for the two ladies.

And they also asked cousin Ken and Maxine if they would like to go to Europe with them, and they agreed. My dad always invited people to go somewhere or do something out of the ordinary. That is what I admired, not just about dad but mom as well. He always was one to step out of the box.

The story of the accident resurfaced when my dad and my mother were on a tour of Europe. As the story goes, he was in a line for a dinner theatre in Paris. True to his nature, he started a conversation with strangers in the queue. Somehow one of the ladies in front of him had a maple leaf brooch on their lapel.

Dad: "you must be from Canada with that maple leaf on your blouse?"

Lady 1: "Yes, we are from Eel Brook near Argyle well. It is actually near the town of Yarmouth...?"

Dad: "Yes, I am from Halifax too and familiar with Yarmouth and Eel Brook."

Lady 2: "What is your name?"

Dad: "Thomas Taylor."

Lady 2: "Oh my gosh, you are quite famous or infamous. However, it goes, in that area. You were the center of an accident for our neighbor, Mr. Johnson, age 95. Small world."

Dad: "I will tell you exactly how it happened from my standpoint.

I was traveling down the highway toward Yarmouth, where I would spend the night. The road was straight, and there was nothing in my path until it was out of the blue; this man walked down the stairs of his house heads for the road to cross to the other side, I suspect. When he came into my vision path, I was sure he would stop and wait for me to pass. Nope, he didn't. So, the next best thing for me was swerving to the right, ending up in the ditch. The older gentleman ended up in the middle of the road, sitting down, with his shoes removed, sitting side by side.

There was a great who ha in the community. There was no one

around until this all happened. Then there were people everywhere. Another traveler driving by hopped out of his car and helped me out of my car to safety. I was more in shock over the incident than anything. I contacted my office, and the office manager Lillian Turner at the time, told me not to say a word to anyone that the head office would handle the press. It was quite an experience. I have to say."

Lady 2: "Well, Thomas, I have to say you are still the talk of the town of Argyle this many years later."

Argyle lies 3 miles or 4.8 km to the southeast of Eel Brook. Eel Brook is where dad had a near-fatal car accident about 65 years ago.

Dad traveled the province of Nova Scotia and Prince Edward Island, so he knows almost every nook and cranny of the two regions. He had a story about every trip he took. Even today, in his 90's, he can recite a story. His memory is pretty darn good. He has had a wonderful life of adventure and intrigue. Most people have not even left their small town to check out the mysteries outside the boundaries, but he was adventurous. He wants to move back to the Maritimes mostly to live in Yarmouth. It has the best climate. He says the weather is probably the best in the country since the Gulf stream is right off the coast of Nova Scotia.

Yarmouth has a humid continental climate of the maritime influence, typical of environments surrounded by the sea but close to large continents such as southern Norway. Of course, there are latitude variations. Being exactly in the -3°C is the average of the coldest month (east of the city), causing that in peninsular areas like Yarmouth Bar and Cape Fourchu. Though owing to solid maritime influences, temperatures below -20°C are infrequent, and the average high rarely drops below freezing at any point in the year.

Dad used to share the highway driving with a dear friend Warren Allen, a traveling salesman. Warren sold roofing products; sometimes, they would take dad's car, and other times they would take Warren's car. The two had so many laughs together and were friends forever. Warren has passed away now, but they always kept in touch after they both retired. We always enjoyed a visit with Warren.

Our oldest daughter Jessica and I had spent a weekend at his place when we traveled from Vancouver to Halifax and needed a place to stay while attending to a close friend of this daughter. His stories were hilarious and unusual as well. Jess and I still chuckle over our weekend adventure with Warren.

When my husband and I moved to the east coast, Warren drove up to our place for a few days on one occasion when my parents were visiting. There were many chuckles and giggles for a few days. While driving, they were usually told crazy stories or read books to one another. It was resourceful when one was driving while the other read a chapter.

I may have already mentioned this, but my dad has been an avid reader.

All my growing up years and up until about three years ago, dad always had at least two books on the go. When he would finish one, he would be on another. He had a friend Kay Scoble, a book supplier, who also recently passed away. Dad also had read the bible many times, cover to cover. A few quite tattered bibles are in the bookcase from reading them repeatedly. I used to supply him with bibles when I owned my little Christian bookstore. In these last few years, he has been reading his Book of Common Prayer for the Anglican church. It is something he keeps in his home and one in the car.

Dad tells another story about when he, Warren, and another chap (Llyod) were with them on one of the trips. There were three single beds in a row, and the three were all tucked in with their jammies when one looked across and observed.

Warren: "Look at that, fellows. We all have the same pajamas on. How can that be?"

Lloyd: "All I can say is our wives shop at the same department store."

Dad said the three laughed so hard that tears were rolling down their cheeks.

Conversations with Dad

On another occasion, when the three were traveling together, Warren was the last one to go to sleep that night. Just before he closed his eyes, he looked around to see that Llyod looked like he was awake.

He told dad, "Look at him. His eyes are wide open, and he is asleep."

Dad knew about this before the three were to share a room this one night.

Dad told Warren that Llyod had had an accident in the war, and he could never close his eyelids. The nerves in the muscles of his eyelids are damaged.

Warren found it a little spooky to have someone sleeping, snoring, and eyes wide open. I have to agree it does sound very creepy. It would be like traveling with your very own Rocky Horror picture show. Maybe everyone doesn't know what that is. The picture was a cult classic, sweethearts Brad and Janet, stuck with a flat tire during a storm, discover the eerie mansion of Dr. Frank'-N-Furter, who was a transvestite scientist. As the innocent unveils his latest creation: a muscular man named none other than "Rocky," hence the name Rocky Horror picture show.

Karen Isis Dad in Fort Langley. BC

CHAPTER 10

Friends and Humor

As the primary salesman for the maritime that did not include Newfoundland, dad also made monthly trips to PEI.

A little trivia!

Charlottetown is the capital and the largest city of the Canadian province of Prince Edward Island and the county seat of Queens County. Named after Queen Charlotte, Charlottetown was incorporated as a city in 1855. It was the site of the Charlottetown Conference in 1864- the first gathering of Canadian and Maritime statesmen to discuss the proposed Maritime union. This conference led to the union of the British North American colonies in 1867, which was the beginning of the Canadian confederation. PEI did not join the league until 1873. From this, the city adopted the motto Birthplace of Confederation. The population of Charlottetown today is about 40,500.

Summerside is another city on the storybook island of Prince Edward Island. It is the second-largest city in the province and the primary service center for the western part of the island. The estimated population is 14,500.

Dad has many wild and beautiful stories about these trips. He sold in the bigger cities, Charlottetown and Summerside, one on the east and one on the west. He did business with Carson and Birt and a glass company right in the heart of Charlottetown. They became fast friends, or you can say, loyal friends. Although many believe that the idiom "fast friends" means friends who developed a liking for one another quickly, the term is a shortened form of steadfast friends. The phrase fast friends come from an even older version of the word steadfast, which means faithful, trustworthy, and steady in adhering to promises or friends in older English. Making friends easily is a trait of dad for sure. The closest ones were the Birts and the Carsons.

Dad: Did I tell you about the times I went fishing and hunting with George Carson?

Me: No, dad, please tell me.

Dad: Back in the day, I visited the island for business. Of course, I was invited to the Carsons as well. George wanted to go fishing some evening, so he asked me to tag along. On a few occasions, his wife Evelyn also came with us. She and I sat either in the car or near the dock where George was fishing. We had some great chats about life and family. They had one son. Then there were the times it would be just me and George going duck hunting. He was the hunter, and I just sat in the car."

There was a time when the Carson and Birt owners offered to sell the business to my dad.

Me: Why didn›t you buy the business from the Carson and Birt group?

Dad: Yes, the two gave me the first opportunity to buy it. I discussed it with your mother and we decided it wasn't a great idea. We loved the island but thought it would be too far from your grandparents. So unofficially, I did buy- not for us but Pilkington Glass Ltd.

Birts were even closer since they had two daughters, one a little older than me and the other a year older, so we had more in common. After all these years, we still are close friends. Mariel and I both wanted to go into nursing. Well, that was what our mothers wanted. We seem to have a great visit every time we get together. Once we met was when my dad was here from the east coast. He so loves this family, he says they are like family. We all met at St. Hubert Chicken restaurant with Mariel, her husband Daryl, Judy (Mariel's sister), and her husband Wayne, son Kevin, and daughter-in-law Cindy. We had a great time catching up and sharing.

We hoped to get over and see them after the pandemic eased up on its restrictions. Dad considers the Birts as family, and we do too. We have a lot of kissing cousins there.

Me: I vividly remember going to Judy›s wedding, and you picked me up after school. I was in grade nine and had to take my books with me? I had to study Latin. The funny, silly things that stick in our minds. We were driving from Halifax to Charlottetown. We left my brother with mom and gran gran. (remember I said earlier those were the names I had assigned to my grandparents.) Remember the gift you gave them? Tell me again. It was ingenious on your part Dad.

Dad: Oh, that was a great wedding. I was the master of ceremonies. Many people, great food and I presented the gift during the reception. Remember what happened?

Me: Oh yes, I do for sure. Tell me again

Dad: well, we were giving the happy couple a crystal tray. I planned for another gift wrapped identically like the actual gift, but with broken glass inside. I presented the gift to Wayne and made sure he dropped it. Crash, bang, crash. Oh, the hush in the hall was deafening. Everyone thought I ruined the gift. Only I knew the truth. Once everyone pulled their chins out of their soup, I brought the actual gift forward and said, « Oh, that wasn›t the gift. That was broken glass from the warehouse. Oh, there was laughter and shock. It was a great trick. And to this very day, the groom said he had pulled the same trick once when he went to a party.»

Dad did that one more time at a Pilkington function. The real gift was a silver tray, and many people in the audience knew that, but when the crash happened, they didn't recall the actual gift.

Me: "oh, dad, remember when Ted Redway had a pet snake in the office one day?"
Dad: « Oh yes, he had a boa in a briefcase that was identical to the boss›s briefcase. He switched the cases when the boss was not looking. He walked away for a time until Mr. Sherman needed to go into his case, and then there was a great commotion, lots of laughter, and the boss shut the lid of the case ever so quickly."

As you have witnessed, my dad loved to pull pranks on other people. But they were pretty harmless. He loves seeing people laugh with good humor and no malicious intent. He was always trying to win friends and influence people. That is a quote from Andrew Carnegie, but that was him too, my dad. We would be walking by a group of people, and there would be little children with their parents, and dad would always try to make the little one's smile. He loved little children. When I watched television with dad, there were commercials or documentaries on television, and he would sometimes say he just couldn't watch it when children were hurt and crying. He was so tender-hearted.

He has a most infectious laugh making everyone around him want to laugh too. He likes to be the center of attention, being a very gracious entertainer.

Me: Dad, do you remember the table dancing trick?
Dad: Oh, this was a fantastic harmless trick at parties. It always seemed like some magic trick, but it was somehow created by the movement of a card table with the presence of energy.»

Conversations with Dad

Dad used to do it near the end of the evening when the party would be at a bit of a lull. There would be a card table, and at least four people would sit around it with their hands on it with lots of pressure, creating a tremendous amount of energy, and then the end is opened for the table to start dancing. Many people think it is hocus pocus, but it is merely electric energy created by hand pressure. Once the table was in motion, dad started to shout, "up table up table." Everyone around him always seemed to enjoy his humor.

Dad is second from the left in his army reserve group

CHAPTER 11

College of St. Ann's Digby NS

My husband and I visited the mysterious school, St. Ann's College, in Church Point, Nova Scotia. It is a beautiful place even now. The administration took me on a small tour. The rooms used as dormitories also come from the classrooms. They are all restored beautifully. It was the place dad was to attend for his Grade 10 level. He thinks his parents have sent him there to curb his wild behavior, which is more likely to get him on track with his studies. They had grand plans for their son.

The school is now used as a bilingual university. The Eudist order of priests established it. In 1890, the Eudists [Congregation of Jesus and Mary] arrived from France to set up an educational institution for Nova Scotian Acadians of Baie Sainte-Marie [St. Mary's Bay]. They also took charge of two parishes in the region. Over the decades that followed (until the 1970s), members of the Congregation would fill the roles of educator, religious community builder, administrator, writer, and even nationalist. Their presence at Point-de-l'Église [Church Point] is an example of a cross-cultural encounter between the French and Acadian communities that left its mark on the region's architectural, cultural, and religious levels. The gradual transition from being a congregation mostly of French priests to one staffed entirely with Canadian clergy created a balance between these two cultural factions within the institution. Over the years, the Eudist contribution to the Nova Scotian French-speaking community's heritage has been expressed in various ways.

During the Third National Convention of Acadians in Church Point, Nova Scotia, they decided to build a college in that town. The location is ideal, right on the ocean.

The college administration was to be assigned to a religious institution, and the Eudist Fathers accepted the challenge. The new educational institution was called Collège Sainte-Anne. As with other schools in Nova Scotia then, students at this college received an education in French and took some courses in English. Collège Saint-Anne became an important educational institution, and several graduates made their mark on Acadian society.

In 1971, the Eudist Fathers decided to hand over responsibility for the College, and it became a non-denominational institution. The college Saint Anne was incorporated as a University Sainte-Anne on April 30, 1892. Two Eudist fathers, Gustave Blanche and Aime Morin were sent from France to found the College.

* * * *

Dad: I remember when the three of us, mom, dad, and me, went with another couple in their car to Hubbard. It was September 3, 1939. I remember that so well. They had a radio in the car, and Prime Minister Neville Chamberlain from England visited Adolf Hitler about an economic proposition. He walked away from the situation with a paper in hand and said, "there is peace in our time." Then, three days later, I was in a movie theatre, and there were the newsreels of Neville with the paper. Then a few days later, there was a news blast stating Germany had declared war on Russia and Europe. It was a world disaster."

That is how dad recalls war days. He was astonished that he remembered the exact date of September 3. He is a fantastic man.

He went on saying: "I can remember exactly what he wore. He always wore a white stiff collared shirt with a black tie. He had no hat on, and he had a handlebar mustache. I remember him being very uptight and severe. He was tall and skinny. I have a picture of the grandparents, who did not look tall or thin.

Dad: When my parents went on a trip to England in 1956, it was quite the affair. They arrived in Liverpool and only were there a few days when my dad dropped dead in the hotel. When the police arrived, my mother told me she mentioned to one of them that dad was a member of the Masons. So, the officer passed this information on to the chief, and he arranged for mom to have a taxi available all the time, and they arranged for mom's return boat trip. She stayed a few weeks longer to make all the arrangements for dad to be transported. Mom, during this stay, went to see cousin Ernie, who was my dad's sister's son in Blackpool. When the police checked my dad's wallet for identification and other information, mom said there wouldn't be much money. He didn't carry much with him. But she was astonished to find out he had a lot of cash but didn't spend much money."

When dad talks about cousin Ernie, he digresses about the time he and my mom went on one of their trips to Europe. They stayed with cousin Ernie, and in the early mornings, mom and Uncle Ernie (this is what I would call him out of respect) stood at the kitchen sink gazing out at the surroundings eating their toast and jam. Mom loved her toast and jam any time of the day. I can envision that too.

"I'm not sure I agree" - a famous quote by my dad. He would say this if someone asked him or anyone a question. I know where he comes from since he was a salesman. I have always believed that if you don't know something, just say, "I don't know." It is better to do that than make something up.

****

Dad traveled to PEI many times a year on business; sometimes, he would take us all along, and sometimes he just took me. I used to stay with Mariel Birt. Those trips were so special to my dad and me.

Sometimes I find this little vinet a little unbelievable. Dad speaks of a man he knew in PEI that was very frugal. (It always cracked me up). He didn't have electricity and turned the oil lamps down in the darkness of the evening and dropped his pants. He did not want to wear out his trousers. It seems a bit Spartan, but these folks lived through the depression and knew how to stretch a nickel. So, this may have been true. Or maybe it must have been my dad's story.

I recall this one Saturday shopping morning. I was about 8.5 years, and my brother was about 1.5 years. The four of us were in the Dominion store grocery shopping for the coming week, and a lady came up to the grocery cart and asked the little girl's name. My brother was the one she meant. He was a beautiful baby, but my parents had left his hair quite long, so people assumed the baby was a girl. My parents corrected the lady's assessment and decided they needed to get my brother's haircut.

There were summers when dad and the Birt family rented a few cabins. We all stayed there for the week. Dad and the other fathers worked in town during the day and then went to the beach. It was usually Stanhope Beach. There are three well-known beaches, Barclay, Stanhope, and Cavendish. They are beautiful to walk and roam in and out for miles along the shore. Cavendish is usually known more since it is nearer Anne of Green Gable's home. A story written by Lucy Maud Montgomery.. My mom never really liked going in the water. She always had a lovely bathing suit but would sit on the sidelines and watch us kids. The behind story is that she was tossed into a lake near her home by her grandfather as a young girl. He did not mean to harm her but hoped she would learn to swim. She was forever traumatized by water. She did go into the hot tubs or in the shallow end of a pool to do aquacise in later years.

Dad age 5 years.

CHAPTER 12

Always wanted to be a salesman!

Dad: "One of our favorite summer holidays was the July first weekend trip with the church group. About 6 or 7 families used to spend every year for about four years in a row. I organized it, for the most part. Each year we went to the same park. It was the Ovens' park located in Cape Breton, Nova Scotia. It has caves; that is where the name the Ovens came from.

There were views from the caves of the Atlantic Ocean. There was an entry fee, but it was well worth it. The families in our group were drawn to the incredible beauty and the peace and serenity it offered. It made this place extremely unique. When we started planning our annual camping trip, we would suggest other sites each year, but the group always gravitated back to the Ovens. Remember Susan; this is where you peddled your sunglasses for 25cents."

Me: "Ah yes, dad, this was stomping ground for my career in public life. I quickly learned to approach strangers and was not afraid to ask them, "would you like to purchase a pair of sunglasses for 25cents?" I still chuckle to myself since that would have been my first job at the tender age of nine."

Dad: "I guess you came upon this honestly since I loved selling so much. That was all I ever wanted to do, and I think I did a pretty good job."

Me: "I agree you were a great provider. Thanks, Dad. I couldn't have asked for a better dad."

Dad: "What was your dream as a child when you grew up?"

Me: "I always wanted to be a teacher when I was a child. I am not sure where it came from. After finishing high school, I could have gone to teacher's college in Fredericton, but I leaned toward nursing and followed in Florence Nightingales footsteps. My cousin Margaret Hamilton was a nurse, and she was the only one. Oh, there was also Peggy Caven, Gwen's sister. She was a nurse and of the same generation as Mom. I went into nursing. I started after high school but wasn't sure then, so I left and didn't enter again until I was a married lady with two little girls. I knew I was ready then, but it was more of a challenge, that was for sure."

Dad: "I knew from a very young age that I wanted to be a salesman. I used to sell the Star Weekly and the Halifax Chronicle Herald. I didn't make much, maybe 2 cents a paper. I remember that the customers were not always that reliable in paying for the subscriptions, and I had to pay upfront for the newspapers and hope that I got paid. There were many times that I was left hanging out to dry. Later in my adult life, I sold advertising for the Chronicle Herald. My mother had hoped I would have completed university. Neither of my sisters did any post-secondary education, so that was her hope. She was disappointed when I decided on sales as a career. It was my passion to sell. I did pretty well and provided well for my family. It was the one thing that surprised me about my mother. Don't get me wrong, I loved her dearly, but she never told others I had a sales job. She said I was only a foreman in the glass shop at Pilkington's. I never said anything but sometimes felt she wasn't all that proud of me. But I did love my mother, and I loved to sell. I was good at it too."

Me: «It is an art; not everyone can sell. You have to have a gift to talk to others freely, and you sure did. Everyone was mesmerized by you when chatting, even in your later years when you were not officially a salesman.»

Me: "Dad, what is one thing you want to be remembered for after you pass away?"

Dad: "I want to be remembered for being kind and compassionate to others, and I think I was and still am now."

Me: "Dad, you have been very kind to others. I have always respected you for that. I am thankful for you, Dad, and I also have to add for mom. I was so fortunate to have you two as parents."

Me: "What were the most memorable experiences you had as an adult? I had to ask you this, dad, and I think I already know your responses."

Dad: "My most memorable experiences as an adult were being married to your mom and then becoming a dad to you and your brother. I was honored to be both."

Me: "I knew you would say this, and I am thrilled to hear you say this. You have been a wonderful father."

Me: "Dad, how did you handle stress as an adult?"

Dad: "I don't believe I blew my top very often. Believe it or not, it was more your mother; she was a quiet little person but when she was tested oh oh look out."

Dad continued

I managed to be able to unwind before I came home. And we had a lot of activities that we participated in, your mom and I. We would be on bowling leagues, curled in the cold weather. We played card games, and we did square dancing with the church group. Our life revolved around the friends we had from the church. I have my church life, my bible, and being a lay reader that was part of the way I destressed. I didn't have much to be stressed about."

Me: "What is your wish for our family?"

Dad: "My wish for my family is that you all get along. I know that isn't always viable in all situations. But do the best you can. I know you will try."

Me: "Dad, what is the one thing we can do to honor you after you've passed away? I don't like to think of this happening, either."

Dad: "Oh, Susan, it is part of life. Death- is going to happen to all of us. But as far as how can you honor me. That is a tricky question to answer. I want you and your brother, of course, to be good people. I know you are good people and try your hardest to continue to do so. I also hope you continue to make your marriage strong to honor us. We had a pretty good marriage, and that is what we also want for you. You and Frank have already had a half-century; maybe you will get another 20 years as your mother, and I did. I pray for you and your families daily."

Baby Isis and Dad

CHAPTER 13

Fond Memories of the Past

We used to play bridge with my parents, and now it isn't the same for him to play bridge since my mom was his partner. The Covid 19 Pandemic made it a little difficult to keep playing bridge. I don't think I played one game of bridge at the Pandemic's height. Hopefully, that will change.

Me: "Dad, when did you start playing bridge?"

Dad: "It was way back when we lived in Saint John, NB. We used to play with Chris and George Gillis. That is where it all began."

"Oh, I must tell you a story of playing golf with George. We belonged to the West field Gold and Country club. George called on a Friday evening and asked if I would like to get off early with him the following day. I agreed. Then Saturday morning rolled around. I was ready to hop in his car, and George said, "Tom, you had better go home and put on your flannel PJ bottoms today. It is mighty chilly on that course today. The Gillis were great friends of ours, as you are aware. You and Chris were friends to the end."

"Thinking of them reminds me of when we went to the Rotary club ball in Saint John. I was all decked out in my finest suit, and your mom looked lovely. Have I told you how much I loved her? I will try and move on without tearing up. When Chris saw me in my beautiful brown suit, she said without hesitation, "oh Tom, you can't wear that. You have to have a tuxedo. George has two, maybe even three. Chris promptly took me into the house and had me change into one of the tuxedos he had hanging in his closet. It was another good night with the Gills'."

Me: "Yes, I remember them so well. One thing of interest was their regular-size black Poodle. His name was Beau, and he lived up to the name."

Whenever the family would head out in the Peugeot, George would be in the driver's seat, Chris would be behind him, and Beau had the place of prominence in the passenger seat. It was quite a sight.

Dad: "It is with great sadness they are all gone except for Peter, their son who lives near you in the Maritime provinces. I always have said I would love to live in the Maritimes, but it would have to be Yarmouth, Nova Scotia. I think the weather there is almost as warm as in British Columbia. I don›t think it would happen now at this stage of my life."

Me: "Perhaps a good idea would be for you to come and stay with us in the spring, summer, and early fall, then return to your condo for the winter. We could even come back for the winter months with you."

Dad: "I may just do that."

My dad's life has had a definite change of events. He was on his own the second Christmas after mom, and we decided to surprise him and arrive on the 27th of Dec. He was so excited about us coming. I didn't inform him until the day of arrival. We rented a car since he wasn't driving. We drove up the road to the condo and noticed Dad approaching us. He was pretty mobile at that time. We planned only to stay for a month and return to our place in NB. We got a call from our older daughter and husband. She said she and her husband had to leave India. The sad part was they had to leave their son behind. It was right smack dab in the middle of the Pandemic, and they had to isolate themselves, but where? So we had a plan that they would isolate in dad's bedroom since he had an on-suite, and the three of us would have the other part of the condo.

Another great feature was the massive balcony that the couple could access from their bedroom, which we could access from the living room. That is just how flexible dad is and was always—stepping up to the plate to help others.

After the two weeks of isolation, we extended our stay another month since we hadn't seen Jess in a long time. It was a great time to visit with Danny. I always call him my favorite son-in-law. He always responds, "I think I am your only one." We always chuckle and smile at his immediate response every time.

The next six weeks were tremendous. Dad loved having us visit and take care of him. He totally denies he needs someone to look after him- part of male pride. He is actually very thankful to have the grandkids, Jess and Dan, to look after him from arm's length.

Dad was born in Halifax Chebucto Road and lived there until he married mom. He moved to Toronto after their wedding and then to Peterborough for a short while.

Dad: "You know, when your mom became pregnant with you, she wanted to move back to Halifax near her parents, which was totally understandable, wishing to be near your parents for their grandchild. We moved to a place in the north of Halifax; I believe it was Robie street. We had a room on the third floor and had to walk down two flights to the bathroom. The availability of places to leave was pretty scarce.

We stayed there for almost a year after you were born, then we moved to a place on Bayers Road. We had two rooms upstairs and had full use of the kitchen, on the main floor. We were good friends of the couple who owned the house, Nora and Doug Valentine. They had no children, so you were very special to them. Did I ever tell you I trained you to go up and down the stairs?"

Me: «Oh, maybe, but tell me again.»

Dad: "You were barely passed a year old and was still drinking from a bottle, so I put the bottle up one step and climbed up and moved your bottom up to get it, and then I would do the reverse down. It worked like a darn. I don't know where I got that idea, but I should put it on youtube today."

Dad: "We soon grew out of the little apartment. Your mom was going to go back to work at Moir's Chocolate factory. No, she didn't fill the chocolates with cherries or caramel flavors. She was the secretary and really enjoyed her job. You had to be taken to your grandparents for the day. So, every day you would go there. You loved your grandparents more."

Me: "Yes, dad, they were the absolute best grandparents anyone could wish for. Oh, dad, I remember when I was playing with all kids in the neighborhood. I distinctly remember one of them was Johnny Rodgers. I always wondered what had happened to him. Maybe I will look him up next time when I am in Halifax. Anyways I am diverting from the story. We were running and laughing and playing with whatever, we could find along the way, and one of the kids picked up a tiny stone and aimed it at the front runner. It didn't hit the front person as intended but the vast plate glass window of the pharmacy on the street corner from my grandmother's place. Oh my goodness, we all were so scared. Everyone stopped in their tracks, made an about-face, and ran for their lives. Yes, everyone except guess who. You guessed it. Me!! I was so surprised about what had just happened, plus my friends left me standing to take the blame. Finally, I did the same thing and ran to grandma's place just like little red riding hood did to get away from the big bad wolf. The staff must have poked their head out the door and saw little Susan running down the street. Everyone nearby knew who I was. They called the local police officer, and he came knocking at the door of grandma's house. By this time, I was clutching grandma. I called her mum. She said she would take care of things for the officer. I was petrified. Meanwhile, I kept telling her, "I will tell Tom." That is what I had called you for a while. Grandma's response was, "go ahead and tell Tom" I still remember saying just that to this day.

Dad: "Oh, I remember that episode. I was called at the office and came right over."

Me: "You were so sweet to me. Mom told you what I had said. "I will tell Tom" We all had a chuckle."

Dad: "I had spoken to the pharmacy owners and said my office would take care of the broken glass immediately. Oh, I remember that. There are some things you never forget, no matter how bad your memory gets. I know I forget some things these days, but I am in my late 90s."

Me: "I keep telling myself it's just a number."

Dad: «Me too.»

Dad enjoying a ice cream cone on Saturna Island, BC

CHAPTER 14

Always a true supporter of me!

Me: "Hey, dad, I vaguely remember where we moved after living with Nora and Doug Valentine. We moved to Fairview just off Dutch Village Road. It was a little two-bedroom house. And there was a backyard but at the far back was another house where my friends lived. The Fredricks. They had two daughters. The older one Nora was my friend most of the time. It was the first day of school, and I thought I would like to go too. I was too young, but I went anyway. Just typical of me, though.

Dad: "Yes, you completed high school, then waited till you had two little girls, and your husband was temporarily out of work before you decided to return to get your nursing."

Me: "Everything has its perfect timing. Then I did my general nursing 30 years later and did my master's in theology and my Ph.D. in counseling by the time I was a senior citizen."

Dad: "Why did you do a master's in Theology?"

Me: "Well, dad, I had enough of nursing technology. I was brought up in the church. Bible studies was one thing, but I thought I studied the bible and better understood why I believe.

Dad: "Brilliant plan."

Me: "Oh, back to the first day of school. I went with Ramona

Fredricks, and she took me to her class." The teacher says," Ramona, who is your little friend? She told the teacher I was her neighbor and friend and said, "she is smart enough to be here." I remember this as if it was yesterday. The teacher was lovely. She said she would call the principal and see what she would have to do. I think they must have called you dad? You reached school in about the next fifteen to twenty minutes."

Dad: "As you know, you must have turned five that year to start school. So, this morning, I was at the office and got a phone call from Mr. Rowe, the principal. He said, Tom, I have your daughter Susan in the office. She isn't in trouble. She just decided to come to school this morning with the little girl who lives next door to you. I would genuinely like to see her stay as I know she is bright enough, but the school rules don't allow it. Can you come and get her? I said, 'Oh, Dave, I would be happy to go and get her. I know she would love to stay.' That is all that happened. The principal was willing to keep you, which would have meant starting school a year early, but the school board didn't allow it. What a silly rule! Too bad I know you were smart enough."

Me: "Thanks, dad. You are a true supporter."

Dad: "So I took you home. Your mother wasn't working that particular day. Those neighbors were so lovely, and we all had so much fun. Do you remember us trying to catch the mouse in that house? We had a Winnipeg couch for a sofa; if you don't know what that is, it is one where you can store blankets underneath, and when lifted, it turns into a double bed. We found that little "sucker" in the bedding under the couch. Your dear little mommy was up on a chair screaming, "Tom, Tom get the mouse." You little timid girl was watching everything your mother did. She was your mentor in many ways since you spent a lot of time with her. To end the story, we caught a mouse and put mouse traps in many of the corners of the house. Your mother immediately wanted to move to another place; that little mouse freaked her out. It was getting to a time when we could almost afford to buy our own house. Well, mortgage it anyway. We didn't quite have enough for a down payment, so my wonderful mother-in-law lent us the money to buy our house on 72 Micmac street. I paid her back. She didn't want any interest, just the money. They were the best.

This house was a two-bedroom house, and only the three of us were there. You were only five years old. The place was lovely, with a big backyard. You had instant friends across the street and next door.

Me: «Oh, I remember Darlene Smith, Doreen Monroe, and the Rouselle sisters Suzanne and Lise."

Dad: "Do you remember we took the Rouselle girls to see the Blue Hawaii movie starring Elvis Presley. You were about ten at the time."

Me: «Oh, I remember that. I had to have the complete recording, and I was not sure if I had an allowance then, but I purchased it with my own money.»

Dad: "What I remember about the movie most was the girls, Lise and Suzanne. There was a part of the movie where Elvis was singing a blues song, or maybe it was nothing but a hound dog. He was shaking his legs and gyrating his body on a stage and singing for all he was worth. I looked over at them, and they both had their eyes covered. I asked them what was wrong? Lise, the older of the two, spoke up and said: 'Oh, the nun at our school and church alike said it was sinful to look at Elvis when he was shaking his body like that or anyone doing it.' I said: 'Oh, I am sorry, girls, we can leave if you like.' 'Oh no, it is alright, we like the movie.' They said together in unison."

It was such a great house. Dad wanted a sunporch built on the house, so when he did this, he put red vertical siding on the front and painted the rest of the house to match. The front room needed a much bigger window, so he had a large picture window installed.

Me: "Do you remember Hilda Armstrong, our next-door neighbor? She was quite an individual. I can still see her over the fence. We had a white picket fence; it was low enough that you could stretch your leg over and didn't have to climb it."

Dad: "That reminds me of the time."

Me: "Dad, are you not going to tell us about the kittens that mom did not want?"

Dad: "Oh, I am afraid so. Minnie, our dear and beautiful calico cat, had five little kittens, and your mother didn't want to raise more kittens or try to find homes for them, so she told me to get rid of them. So, I always did what your mother said."

Me: "Well, that is another story!"

Dad: "So I went next door to Hilda's place and said, 'Hilda would you be able to get rid of these little kittens?' Hilda replied, 'Oh, no problem, Tom, I will get a bucket of water.' She picked them up one by one and sang a song as each one was submerged in the cold water. It went something like this You always hurt the one you love, the one you never want to hurt. The next thing I knew was that five little dead kittens were lying on the ground. Hilda said, 'Well, Tom, it is up to you now to get rid of them.' So I had to bury the little darlings."

Me: "I know what happened next. It was about 4 pm, and I had just returned home from school. I went to the back door and caught you burying the little darlings. I was so upset. You put your arms around me and said you were sorry, but we couldn't keep all five kittens. I got over it slowly. Oh, and once when you came home from work, let Minnie out the front door. That was an alright thing to do. Minnie went out the front door and returned to the back door. But this particular day, a car was racing down the road when Minnie was crossing the street, and boom hit our Minnie. We were in the house and had no idea until the doorbell rang. All my friends knew our Minnie. They came and said Mr. Taylor look at Minnie. Oh, we were devastated. We loved that beautiful cat. You once again had the task of disposing of this furry body lying in the middle of the street. The driver who hit the kitty didn't stop to say sorry but just kept going. I know you didn't want to bury her, so you called the city, and they sent out a giant dump truck in about 20 minutes. It was a good thing it wasn't any longer because 12 little children were crying their eyes out. The dump truck pulled up, picked up the cat by her tail, swung it around, and tossed her into the truck, and he immediately drove away. The kids blamed you for the cat being hit. It indeed wasn't you causing an accident."

Dad: "I felt horrible, really horrible."

We still talk about poor little Minnie.

Dad was playing a Judge in a play. looks pretty good!

CHAPTER 15

MicMac Street

Behind our house was a large empty field bordering low-cost housing. I had a few friends who lived here since we went to the same school. But the family I remember most was the Dewitt family. There were four children—Ruby David, Ronnie and lastly Bobby. Bobby was the funny happy kid in the family, always playing tricks on everyone. He always reminded me of a goofball.

Me: "I wonder what ever happened to that family. I know Ruby became a nurse and worked at the Victoria General in Halifax, eventually getting married. Other than that, have no idea—we lose touch with people."

Dad: "I remember them. We used to drive them to church every Sunday until we moved to Connaught Avenue."

Me: "Hey, Dad, do you remember how I used the window for my good?"

Dad: «What are you referring to?»

Me: "I was about six years old, and I had these red spots on my body, and of course, we figured they were measles, but mom thought it would be best to go to the doctor. Our doctor was a gruff old guy. He had minimal bedside manners, but he was a good doctor, which is what mattered most. He took one look at the spots and said she would be fine. Just keep her from watching television. We were one of the only families on Micmac street at the time who had a tv, so we were more fortunate. When we got home, we had supper, and the three of us sat to watch television for the evening. Mom said, 'no, no, you must not; that is what Dr. Graham told us.' I turned and looked out the huge picture window, and guess what; there was a reflection of what was on tv. I wasn't a pretty face, was I?" (ha-ha)

Dad: "I at first couldn't fathom why you were so complacent about not being able to watch 'my three sons,' one of our favorite shows. Then a light bulb went on. I could see you watching the show in the reflection. I knew then you were a pretty smart cookie."

Me: "Oh, dad. Anyone would have done that." Smiles.

Mom had used the house for election stations during a few provincial and federal elections. She was a pretty resourceful lady.

Me: While living in that house I was close to my grandma's. She lived at #3, and we lived at #72. So, after school, I used to stop there and walk up Bayers Road. My friend Jane Foley and I would walk together she would leave to go into her house and I would continue to Grandmas' place.. They lived in a lovely place like our next house on Connaught Avenue.

Dad: "Yes, I was friends with her dad Brian Foley and her mom Eileen was a lovely lady, but she had problems with depression."

Me: "I remember now what you are referring to. One night the father went out with his friends, and when he returned, he found the two of them had passed away in the closet. The mother had shot Jane and then herself and they were in the closet. It must have been so devastating for him to find them and then be all alone. I know I couldn't walk on the same side of the street for a long time. I changed my path, crossed over at the school's bottom, and then walked to the top by Margaret Coxes' house so I would not have to walk in front of the house.

Dad: «I never knew you went through that. But it makes total sense to a nine-year-old child.»

The one thing I didn't really like about living on Mic Mac

Street was there were only two bedrooms. Now that is a first-world problem. Some kids have to share a room with their parents or with five or more siblings. But it was different. When my brother was born, it was a novelty at first as I quite liked to brag, I had a brother and never told many people how much younger he was than me. After his first year or two, we shared a bedroom. Mom and dad took mine, which wasn't too small for a single room, and my little brother and I were together. He was pretty young because one of the times we shared the room, he was in a crib.

Dad: "Oh, I remember that. We changed the rooms around a lot, back and forth, moving the furniture. That is one pheromone of your mother that was quite prevalent. She loved to update the furniture in the house. I had to ensure I turned the bedroom light on before entering the room. It would be no surprise to find the bed or the dresser by the door in a different place. The living room was constantly being changed around. That may be why she always wanted to move to get a different perspective on her house. We seemed to move a lot. But I recall you and your brother sharing a room from time to time until he was about three or four. Then, you started getting a lot of homework and needed peace to study. So, you were granted the privacy of your own room again, and that was the last time you had to share a room."

Me: "Oh, this must have been when you bought that grand house on Connaught Avenue- two doors up from St. Phillips Church and right behind the minister's house."

Dad: "Yes, that is precisely it. We looked around a lot, and this house came for sale. It had three bedrooms. It was a perfect place; the only downfall was you had to change schools. I got permission from the superintendent of schools to have you stay there and finish the year at St. Andrew's school.. It was the best way. You walked to school most days, but on others, I would drive you on my way to the office. Now it was the opposite direction, but it made sense to ensure you were safe. You were my little girl, and I didn't want anything wrong to happen to you."

Living at 3080 Connaught Avenue was great. It was like the Jefferson moving up town. I never thought of it at the time, but when I reflect, it was a little upscale. The great thing was dad got so involved in activities at the church- except for the square dancing from the school; he had to go to a hall near Windsor Street. Having access to the church was great.

The Cooper family behind us, we were great friends with the minister and his family. They had four daughters and, finally, a son.

Dad: «You were friends with the three older girls, and then the fourth girl was the same age precisely as your brother.»

Me: "It was interesting how we could walk to the back of the garage and through the opening in the fence and right to the church or Cooper's house."

Dad: "Remember how I made a room up in the attic for your brother. Your mom thought we should rent out a room, so we created another floor in the house, and it was your brother's room on the entire top floor. It was just the attic completed as a large bedroom. For a while, his access to the room was through your room. It drove you nuts. The stairs were in your closet. So, we remedied that we closed off the staircase and opened up another staircase in the hallway so you had your privacy and little bro had his too. The other bedroom housed a few female roomers while we lived there."

Me: "Oh, I remember Miriam Grant. She was such a beautiful girl. She worked at the navy base as a secretary. And, she fell in love with one of the sailors on the base- Bruce Llewyn. He was handsome too. We all got to be involved with her family. Bruce proposed to her, and then she decided to have a wedding. Miriam asked if we could arrange a marriage here at the house. We obliged as we loved Miriam. She was from Digby, and her father was a church pastor there. He was going to perform the ceremony, and the entire family was coming from Digby. The most unforgivable thing happened the night before the wedding. We were all asleep, and the phone rang. It was Bruce. He called to say he didn't want to get married. He said sorry and hung up. Miriam was devastated."

Conversations with Dad

Dad: "I remember that too. Oh, it was a horrible thing to do. But in retrospect, it was better to do it before they got married, and what a fiasco that would be. Your mom had organized food and a place in the backyard for the guests to sit and later a place to eat where they would be able to mingle. She managed the entry and exit of the house for the washroom and more food. That was all put to rest."

Me: "Miriam was in bits crying all night long. I could hear it from my bedroom. I was only about 13 or 14. Not sure, but it was a poor thing. She quit her job shortly after and moved back to Digby. We never heard from her again. I tried to look her up in 2021 when Frank and I were on a road trip to find St. Anne's college in Digby. No one had heard of the family. Probably I hadn't heard of them because they were not churchgoers, or maybe it wasn't in Digby exactly where she lived."

All the family Jess, Karen, Frank Mom Dad.

CHAPTER 16

Courting my mom

Mom was the love of his life and after her passing and until this very day he never has a day he doesn't include her in his conversation. I may have repeated this statement but whenever he wants to eat, he will say "you know what your mother would say, "and of course I would play into his story telling and reply

Me. No. What would she say dad? "Reservations of course" So he does repeat this scenario lots and lots and it is very cute.

Their relationship was a beautiful love story. He tells me he knew on the first date he wanted to marry her but waited till their third day.

Dad and Mom

Me: Where did you first meet mom?

Dad. We were both working at the Chronicle Herald. Your mom was the secretary/receptionist. And I was an advertisement salesman with the Herald. I would work one night a week and when I was finished, she would pay me 2.40cents for the 1 ½ hours I had worked in the evening. It wasn't much money in today's standards but that was 1947.

Me: How long did you date before you got married?

Dad: Met in May and we were married in November as you know.

Me What did you do on your first date?

Dad: Oh, my lovely daughter I really blew it on our first date.

Me How did you do that dad?

Dad: I made plans to go out the night before and got into a car accident with a group of my mates. The mates were all people I worked with at the Garrick theatre. There was Leo Deveau assistant manager, two projectionists, I didn't tell you I wore a uniform as an usher, it was basically blue with red trim, and I would wear dark trousers. Fortunately the police were not involved but I ended up in hospital overnight and lost three of my teeth in the process. If the truth be known I did have a little too much to drink. I didn't call or let your mother know what had happened for some time.

Me: how long before you called her?

Dad it was coincidence actually I was selling real-estate and your mother called our office and I ended up being the person to show her parents and her the property It was the house on Almond street.. At that time, I asked her if she would be willing to try again for a first date. It is obvious that she said yes.

Me: why did you pick the 20th of November, and it was a Tuesday. I looked it up on the google calendar.

Mom loved it when I would have my cell phone with me, and we were stuck on the answer to something obvious and beyond our memory at the time.

Dad: Well as you are well aware your mother had a perpetual admiration for the British Royal family and so we were married on the same day as the Queen (she was the Princess at the time) and the exact same time.

Me: That seems a little over the time but it is no different than the followers of Elvis who think he is still in the building somewhere, or the fans of George Michael and many more icons.

Dad: it was a lovely affair

Me: What did you do on your dates well at least where did you go on a date?

Dad and Mom Christmas Morning. 1985

Dad: well quite often we would go to the movies, The Oxford Theatre, corner of Oxford street and Quinpool Road. You remember going there don't you?

Me Of Course I do we were close enough to we could walk from our place on Connaught Ave. Where else did you go on a date?

Dad: We would take the street car from her place on Almond street to Point Pleasant Park,. We would take long walks in the park it was quite lovely. I was a bit of a romantic I guess. That's where we would go years later with the church families tobogganing. Do you remember that? We would walk and talk and just get to know each other.

Me: Did you ever double date with anyone? Your friends or mom's friends?

Conversations with Dad

Dad: Well yes we did as a matter of fact. Funny you should say that. We went with Jean Willams who was our bridesmaid and Jim Shaw. Jean was an aide child who lived at Mrs. Decker's house in Jordan Bay NS, until she was 18 and had completed her high school diploma. You may ask what is an aide child well she or he were wards of the court or what we call foster children today. We would mostly go to the theatre or out for dinner. Mind you there were not many restaurants in the day.

Me do you remember the names of any of them?

Dad: Let me think for a few minutes you must remember I am in my mid 90's and struggling to remember what day it is some days. There was the Auction House on Argyle Street, The Press Gang on Princess Street, and oh yes there was Edna's Place on Gottingen Street. This street was the popular shopping area when I was kid and would go shopping on Thursday nights with the entire family. Oh darn I think I already told you this.

Me Oh dad I don't get tired of hearing about all your goings and comings. You are my hero. You knew that already right Dad!

What did mom Say when you asked her to marry you?

Dad: I asked her on the third date as I said previously and she said slow down Tom. I have to ask my parents first. I think she prepared them for it. When they did ask her they both broke down and wept. They were so happy for her and me I think so. There was another step I had to go through. I had to meet the grandparents. That was a trip to Jordan Ferry. It was a bit tricky since I still didn't have my own car as yet. So what happened was my future mother in law asked her husband for the car keys to their car and I drove to Jordan Ferry to meet them. This was an experience I will not forget. The grandparents were very nice and they were people who had raised your grandmother. You know the story of how she was the youngest of 7 children and her mother died in childbirth. So when she was about 4 or 5 the Mitchels became her legal gradians. They never officially adopted her but we all considered them as family

Dad and mom on Alaska Cruise

Me What about your family dad?

Dad: For some unknown reason they didn't take to your mother or her family. We did go to my parent's house before we were married and it was a disaster to say the least. My oldest sister Margaret was quite brutal, verbally to your mother, you see my sister Margaret was a fairly large women and your mother Margaret was very tiny. So she belittled her and critiqued her eating habits and her size. Your mother never really cared to go there again. There was a time when we were dating that I and your mother were walking along Robbie Street and across the street from us was my sister Margaret and we crossed over to say hello and introduce her. Sister Margaret never acknowledged either of us and we three continued to walk the same way and when we got to Almond Street sister Margaret kept going. This interaction was prior to the dinner at my family's house. We didn't react or talk about my family much.

Me: Let's focus on happier things like the actual wedding day?

Dad: I can remember that day as if it was yesterday. I was so in love with your mother. The service was held at St. Mathias church and the reception was at the Lord Nelson hotel. It was just a light lunch but it was beautiful. We only had about 50 people present.

Me: Did you go on a honeymoon right away?

Dad: we stayed in the Lord Nelson Hotel our first night then we went on the greyhound bus to Boston the next day. I still didn't have my own car.

Me: It sounds like you always made the best of every situation.

Dad: I tried to do just that and still do as a rule.

Me That is one of the many things I appreciate and love about you dad.

Mom with her Dad (Oscar) and mother (Ella)

CHAPTER 17

Conversations with my dad Last chapter

I call this the last chapter but really not his last chapter. He is 95 at the time of the creating of this book which was and is a tribute to his strength of character. He plans to live to a 100 and hope he does.

There are so many things I haven't said about my dad. He. Has been a mentor and friend and a confidante to me. His whole life centres around the family and us all working together. There were not many things I would do with out asking his opinion first and the same goes when my mother was alive. I had the utmost respect and love for these two people.

He was such a trivia buff a wealth of knowledge to me. There were times I would be somewhere and someone would ask me a question or we would be doing some project and not know the answer to a question. I would say ". Wait let me call my dad" he just seemed to know a lot of information. This had a lot to do with him being an avid reader. A wonderful trait to have. I mentioned earlier in this book about him having up to three books on the go at any one time. One in the bathroom, that was a given, one in the living room and one by his bedside. OH I forgot the car. In one of those locations of course there would have been a bible. He reads his bible constantly. It was and is his daily guide to life.

Today is a little different since he sits and ponders about his memories with my mom. So he does read a little but mostly shorter articles in the Vancouver Sun or the Province newspaper. The most likely book he would read is the Book of Common Prayer. There are several of those around the house. Oh also in the back pocket in the car too.

What would be a normal day for dad these days?

He sleeps til 8.00 and then he lays in bed and listens to his religions leaders speak. There are such speakers as John MacArthur, Charles Stanley, Chuck Swindol and of course I think his favourite is David Jeremiah.

A funny thing about his alarm clock, it goes off at the most in opportune times and he will just let it ring and ring. The only way to stop it is to pull the plug. I am not sure why he doesn't change the time or stop the darn thing from ringing. I have heard it go off in the middle of the night but he just leaves it. I do know he has really good hearing. I think he just sleeps thru it, a real gift.

He is a very lucky man. He may not totally agree since he doesn't have the love of his life with him. Other than this very large factor his life has been pretty darn good. He has had two fabulous children, I being one of them of course. He had a family from his origin that doted on him, as he was the youngest and he had two older sisters. He had a wife who waited on him as they say hand and foot, funny expression and then he was very fortunate because he loved his job. He was a salesman all his life and said that is all he wanted to do from a small child is sell and he did it well. He was top salesman for Pilkington Glass a giant glass manufacturer out of St. Helen's, England. To this day it is not owned by a Japanese company. He still receives his pension and excellent benefits from them. He had what we all thought good health until he was told by his doctor he must loose weight or he was going to have a heart attack. So the entire family had to go on a diet with him. It was rice, salad and tuna

Conversations with Dad

for us all. Oh did I mention skim milk too. He was very diligent with the new regime and did manage to get his weight down but not soon enough since about 10 years later he was at work. It was a warning heart attack and was put on an exercise program and new eating changes were in the works as well. It was a known fact that he ate very rich food when he travelled with his job so that in it self contributed to the unhealthy heart. He was pretty active but not in the physical sense. He was always on the go socially and taking us places since our mother didn't always drive. When she started to drive so did I so it was a bit of a Russian roulette with the car. That is we always took our chances waiting for dad to come home.

So it was after this that he became very healthy and we all were on his plan. My husband chuckles about coming over to eat at our place and there would be nothing but rice, fish or tuna. That is a little bit of an exaggeration but pretty close. I never knew that he felt that way. Hence I smile to myself just thinking about this.

So many years later he had open heart surgery when he moved to British Columbia the year of 9/11 and that was probably the best thing he could have done to prolong his life. He still continues to watch his diet and he walks well for a tall man in his mid 90s and no cane until recently when he did take a tumble and now the entire family has encouraged him to use a waking stick It is an old style the cane which he calls a walking stick. Which is a little more of a fashion statement. So there have not been many major things happen aside from open heart surgery and that was over 20 years ago and he is still kicking. He is a lucky man.

We are also very lucky to have our dad and grandfather all these years. He is a blessing to all of us. Thanks Dad for all you have done. I know he would y say he has done nothing more than any other father but we know for sure that is now true.

We love you Dad!

P.S. Dad was chatting with me on the phone the other night after Queen Elizabeth passed away and told me the story of how he and mother, who had a list of all the stops the Queen !! Was making on her 1951 tour to Halifax. They basically chased the Queen's entrouage around the city of Halifax. He had nine other ladies in this two door car. He ended story by saying "the things I would do for your mother"

Me and Dad April 2,1955 walking across the Angus L Mac Donald bridge.

CPSIA information can be obtained
at www.ICGtesting.com
Printed in the USA
JSHW022241260123
36895JS00002B/125

9 798765 235300